A PIECE OF MY MIND

Other books by
EDMUND WILSON

I THOUGHT OF DAISY

CLASSICS AND COMMERCIALS

MEMOIRS OF HECATE COUNTY

TO THE FINLAND STATION

THE SHORES OF LIGHT

AXEL'S CASTLE

POET'S FAREWELL

THE AMERICAN JITTERS

TRAVELS IN TWO DEMOCRACIES

THE TRIPLE THINKERS

THE SHOCK OF RECOGNITION

EUROPE WITHOUT BAEDEKER

NOTE-BOOKS OF LIGHT

THE WOUND AND THE BOW

FIVE PLAYS

THE SCROLLS FROM THE DEAD SEA

RED, BLACK, BLOND AND OLIVE

A PIECE OF MY MIND

Reflections at Sixty

by

EDMUND WILSON

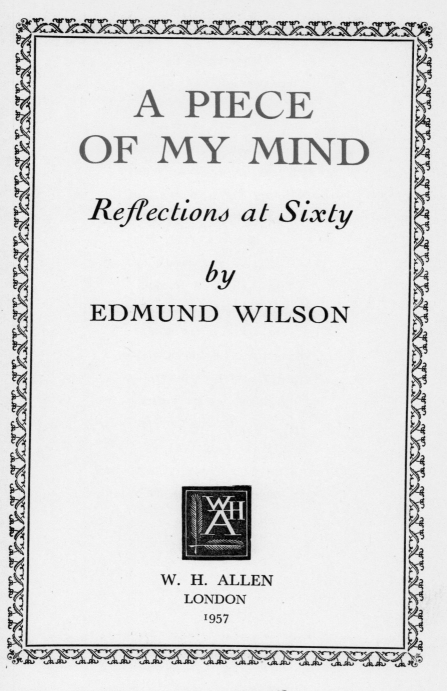

W. H. ALLEN
LONDON
1957

MADE AND PRINTED IN GREAT BRITAIN BY
THE GARDEN CITY PRESS LIMITED,
LETCHWORTH, HERTFORDSHIRE

CONTENTS

I

Religion

RELIGION IS THE CULT of a god, or gods, conceived in supernatural terms. The "religion of humanity" and the "religion of art" are not religious at all, and it confuses the whole question of religion seriously to use such phrases. It is also misleading to talk as if a mere liking or respect for the ritual or the mythology of one of the Christian churches were equivalent to a religion. One may understand Christianity as a phenomenon of human history, admire the productions of Christian art, appreciate the value of this cult in the past, and, for some, at the present time, as a discipline and an inspiration; but to do this is not religion. The *religion* of "Christ" demands that we accept the virgin birth of Jesus and regard him as the true Messiah, literally the son of God, begotten by the Holy Ghost and sent to atone for the sins of men and make possible human salvation; as the performer of unquestionable miracles, who was able to revive the dead and who rose himself from the tomb. We must believe that he sits now at the right hand of God and will preside at a Judgment Day, when the saved shall be winnowed from the damned. We must acknowledge that this Father, Son and Holy Ghost constitute a mysterious Trinity, which, without understanding, we must worship. I am aware that it is not obligatory—not even, I am told, in the Episcopal Church—literally to believe all this. It is permitted to accept some features or even the whole of the creed as true only in a "symbolic" sense. But this is surely to beg the question. If the Saviour is but a symbol, why should we be called upon to worship him? Why should we be asked to build churches and to take the communion in them? The watered-down Christian doctrines—from liberal Episcopalianism to Unitarianism—have hardly more in common with genuine religion than has the "religion" of social service. They are phases in the struggle of modern man to get rid of his genuine religion, to liquidate the old cult of Jesus as a supernatural being.

.   .   .

The New Testament is vague enough and inconsistent enough to lend itself to a variety of interpretations; but certainly the teaching of Jesus, as variously reported in the Gospels, is mainly in the direction of abnegation, of forgiveness, of non-resistance. If there really is a Christian ethics, it is the kind of thing preached by Tolstoy and of which, by his own behaviour, he illustrated the impracticability. There are people, a very few people—Tolstoy was conspicuously not one of them—whose temperament has some affinity with this version of the Christian ideal; but this ideal is, even for them, incompatible with the conditions of human life. The saint says, "So much the worse for these human complications, embarrassments"; mortifies or tortures the flesh or breaks it by succumbing to martyrdom. But the rest of us cannot do this : we must feed and defend ourselves, try to make sure of the survival of our species; and if we admit that this ideal is the Christian one, it is ridiculous to call ourselves Christians. We must constantly—in an infinite variety of ways—be contending with one another, and the attitude enjoined by Jesus would render impossible, not merely war, not merely business competition, but even a vigorous argument, a competitive examination or the rivalry of two men for a girl.

Thus, to take Christianity seriously is contrary to common sense, and of course it has rarely been attempted. In the meantime, the barbarous conflicts between nations that call themselves Christian and invariably invoke the Christian God have been a scandal of such proportions that it has always made insignificant the protests of the saints and the satirists. The morality attributed to Jesus has had perhaps a limited validity in restraining us from unnecessary ruthlessness—though the notion that all men are brothers and should be merciful to one another was not invented by Jesus; but, if generally put into practice, it would prevent any kind of achievement except that of such unusual people as St. Francis of Assisi.

.   .   .

I dwell here upon Christianity simply because it is the dominant religion in the part of the world where I live; but for all the religions the case is the same. They are, of course, not merely impostures, as the eighteenth century sceptics liked to think—not even mere legends and myths, which, as the anthropologists show, are likely to have much in common in however remote parts of the world for the reason that they are all trying to deal with typical situations of human beings in connection with the earth, with the elements, with the forces they feel in themselves and with their relations to one another. They have become, in a sense, realities in the lives of the people who practise them. The resurrection of Adonis or Jesus serves not merely to celebrate the coming of spring, nor is it, for the worshippers of these gods, merely a ritual "symbol" : it can hardly be dissociated from the revival of morale in the celebrants. In the same way, the sacred dances performed by the American Indians may not be accompanied or followed by the rain that the celebrants invoke, but they help to keep up the tribe's spirits during the period when no rain is falling; they represent a dynamic experience of which faith in the rain god is part. The power of prayer is real : when the Arab repeats his ritual, he is sustaining the discipline of his way of life; when the Protestant Christian appeals to his God, he is rallying his own moral forces. But the ecstasy of revival, the strengthening of discipline, the summoning of moral resources are by no means inseparable from the formulas of religion. They are phenomena with which everyone, surely, is more or less familiar. For some, they are made easier by ritual; but for others, they are weakened or degraded by being entangled with folklore or with theological systems, with the practices of primitive people attempting to propitiate the elements or with the imaginative constructions of the learned, aghast at the infinitudes of the universe or the conflicts of impulse in themselves. As for the moments of divine revelation, the direct apprehensions of God, that the saints and the prophets describe, unbelievers have no right to deny them. The ecstasy of imaginative vision, the sudden insight into the nature of things, are also experiences not confined to the religious. The scientist and the artist know them. But they talk about them in other terms.

. . .

The word *God* is now archaic, and it ought to be dropped by those who do not need it for moral support. This word has the disadvantage of having meant already far too many things in too many ages of history and to too many kinds of people, along with the disadvantage that the one thing these various meanings have all had more or less in common is an anthropomorphic picture. In the case of the conceptions of the metaphysician—such as Whitehead's "principle of concretion" in the universe—in which the anthropomorphic image tends to disappear, this term seems far-fetched and uncalled-for; and in the case of the ordinary man, it is lazy to use it to designate the impetus which rouses him up from bed in the morning, sends him about his business and makes him believe that that business is important, as well as to provide a "first cause" for the force that sets the ions of physics revolving around their nuclei and the planets around their suns. There is no classical conception of God that can really be made to fit what we know today, in the middle of the twentieth century, of the behaviour of what we call "energy" and the behaviour of human beings, and of the relation of these to one another. Yet we still use the word in this indolent sense to cover up our inability to account, in a "rational" way, for the fact that we exist, that the universe exists, and that everything is as it is. At some point in the distant past, human beings became aware that their bodies had been developed in an intricate and remarkably effective way, and since they could not remember having planned this or worked it out themselves, they came to the conclusion, as Paley did—thinking in mechanical terms—that where one found what one took for a clock, there must previously have been a clockmaker. Today such conceptions are obsolete. Though we still make mechanical models of the movements of the planets and the fission of the

atom, we do not see the world as an immense machine. We do
not speak of unvarying scientific laws; we speak of "statistical
averages." We have been forced to recognize the "organic," to
admit that what we used to call "reason" may land us in a cul-de-
sac. Yet we keep on performing experiments which we observe
from the rational point of view of the cause that produces the
effect, and we know that we can find out certain things in this
way: techniques for procuring results. What is behind the processes involved? What is involved in our wish to control them?
We do not know. The best we can say is that the universe is not a
machine, set going by a machine-maker, God, but an organism
that is always developing, in which we, interrelated with everything else, have our life-cycles as unified groups of impermanently
clustering particles. But to say that all this was created by "God"
or to identify it somehow with "God" is to supplement our human
ignorance with a gratuitous fairy story. As we come to understand
more and more about the processes of "life" and "matter," we
discover that it is less and less easy to differentiate clearly between
them. As we probe into the happenings in the universe—electrical
and cerebral phenomena, the transit of light waves and sound
waves, the multiplication of cells in organisms, the inherited
combinations of genes—we find them, to be sure, less amenable
to the "laws" of the old-fashioned scientist who thought in
mechanical terms. But we do not find a God.

.   .   .

Nor is it possible any longer for us to make the old-fashioned
distinction between man and the lower animals which enabled us
to claim for ourselves something noble we called the "soul" which
the other animals did not have, and to hold ourselves responsible
to a Deity of whom the other animals had no knowledge. Even
minds that rejected this Deity and that questioned the conception
of the human "soul" were inclined to maintain a distinction
between the "reason" of man and the "instinct" of the lower
animals. This distinction is no longer tenable. The discovery of
primitive man and of the kinship of man with the anthropoids
brought at first—in the nineteenth century—along with the
acknowledgment of this kinship, a certain very firm insistence that

৩ 11 ৩

even the anthropoid mammals be made to keep their distance from man. The distinction between "reason" and "instinct" was a part of this holding them at arm's length, as was also the resolute emphasis, on the part of certain schools of thought, on the distinction, in man himself, between "human" and "animal" elements.

If we had to be cousins of the apes, we would, nevertheless, make it clear that the social distance between us amounted to a difference of kind. The point was also pressed at this time that man was the "tool-making" animal. No animal except the human was supposed to use extraneous objects to help it to accomplish a purpose, let alone to shape an object for this purpose. But then it was discovered that the animals did not only the first but the second—and that not only could the mammals perform such feats, but also the insects, the fish and the birds. There is the wasp that picks up a pebble to tamp down the earth on the hole in which she has laid her eggs; there are the fish that shoot down winged insects with perfectly aimed drops of water; the birds that build bowers as well as nests, for reasons that are not known, and black them with pieces of charcoal; there is the anthropoid chimpanzee which not only opens doors with keys and fits hollow reeds together in order to construct a pole long enough to knock down a banana but can even be taught to sew and to eat with a knife and fork. It has sometimes been claimed by persons who have lived on close terms with the higher apes that these latter show certain signs of possessing a "moral sense," and lepidopterists have sometimes imagined that a kind of æsthetic sense is manifested in the patterns of butterflies, which were originated for mimetic protection but have occasionally been carried so far, through a love of elaboration, as eventually to attract attention and expose their creators to danger. We know now that the bees have evolved a code—not of sounds but of movements and stances—by which a scout who has been looking for honey can convey, on his return to the hive, exactly how far away it is and in what direction it lies. Thus the lower animals are very much closer to us than they were to the men of Darwin's time. The old-fashioned dog-lover who could not believe that his pet did not have a soul and who hoped to find him in Heaven may be comforted by some of the findings of the present-day zoologist—though the latter has reduced to absurdity the old-fashioned idea of Heaven, which, if open to dogs, really ought to be open to bees, ants and wasps as well, and has undermined the old-fashioned idea of God, who made man in his image, a "thinking being."

Notes on the Churches

As a result of having published a little book on the subject of
the Dead Sea scrolls, I have recently been brought into contact
with the various Christian churches and have had pointed up for
me their various attitudes towards the faith that they all profess.
It seemed to me that the discovery in these pre-Christian documents of a doctrine, a ritual and a discipline very similar to those
of Christianity, as well as of a "Teacher of Righteousness" who
seemed in some ways to anticipate Jesus—and the finding of these
documents in a corner of the world where John the Baptist began
his ministry and to which Jesus came to be baptized—might
present an embarrassing problem to any theology based on the
dogma that Jesus was the Son of God, a unique and supernatural
figure. I was to some extent correct about this, as the reaction in
certain quarters has shown; yet the scrolls have proved not to be
disturbing to the clergy of so many churches or to so many people
in any church as I had thought they were likely to be.

Dr. Frank M. Cross, Jr., of the McCormick Theological
Seminary in Chicago, an extremely able young scholar who had
been working on the Dead Sea scrolls in the Rockefeller Museum
in old Jerusalem, reviewing my book in the *New York Times* of
October 16th, 1955, rather surprised me by expressing himself as
follows: "In a summary sentence, Mr. Wilson maintains that it
would seem an immense advantage for cultural and social intercourse—that is, for civilization—that the rise of Christianity should,
at last, be generally understood as simply an episode of human
history rather than propagated as dogma and divine revelation.
To anyone trained in Christian theology—not to mention the
English language—this sentence is unintelligible. The terms 'rise of
Christianity' and 'dogma' do not belong to the same universe of
discourse, so that no theologian, or philosopher for that matter,

would dream of propagating one as the other; and no one denies, least of all the Christian, that the rise of Christianity is 'simply an episode of human history.' But never mind. What Mr. Wilson is struggling to say, presumably, is that he wishes that people would give up the theological interpretations of human history; that on reading the scrolls, the Christian will properly give up his faith once he understands that the primitive Christian community had direct connections with its Jewish past, and that its world view, institutions and so on, are derived from or at least have continuity with the historical milieu of the first century A.D. in Palestine. The presumption is that Christian doctrine regards revelation as the suspension of the normal historical process. The author is merely expressing a confusion common to the era of the fundamentalist-modernist fights of a generation ago. And it is true that Christians (or, *mutatis mutandis*, Jews) who share his confusion will be badly shaken up as the implication of the scrolls are spelled out. On the other hand, those acquainted with contemporary theology or with critical biblical scholarship are well aware that the events conceived in Christian (or Jewish) dogma as 'acts of God' are continuous with, and indistinguishable from other events of history so long as they are viewed by the historian as history. Indeed, the Christian doctrine of revelation means just this, that God chooses to give meaning to history, not to suspend it."

I wondered how such Christian dogmas as the Virgin Birth and the Resurrection could be described as "continuous with and indistinguishable from other events of history," and, having occasion to correspond with Dr. Cross in connection with another matter, I asked him about this and received from him the following answer, which I print here with his permission. It seems to me of special interest as a frank and concise statement on the part of an ordained scholar—Dr. Cross is a Presbyterian—in regard to central problems of the Christian faith.

"I must confess that your point on the Virgin Birth and Resurrection would hold in the church at large, especially in Roman Catholicism. It does not hold among other post-liberal theologians writing today : Bultmann, Tillich, Niebuhr, Barth, etc., etc. Neither the Virgin Birth nor the Resurrection is an historical event. But they fall into different categories somewhat. The virgin birth is a late legendary accretion, contradicted by earlier sources who maintain a Davidic ancestry through Joseph. Mark, Paul, proto-Luke and probably John know nothing of it. Theologically it may be meaningful if taken as poetic fancy pointing to the Church's faith that the Christ was born 'under the power of the Holy Spirit,' i.e., in a plan of redemption. If taken as an 'historical' proof of divinity, it is theologically offensive. The legend may have background in such passages as Psalms ii. 7, Isaiah lxvi. 9, and especially II Samuel vii. 11 . . . and in the general Semitic tradition of referring to royalty as 'sons of God(s).' In any case, the historian must dismiss it as unhistorical.

"The resurrection falls into a different category, at least in theological analysis. It is not an historical *(historisch)* event, but an eschatological *(geschichtlich)* event. Like Creation and the End, it has not a direct, but a dialectical relation to history. Inexactly put, the resurrection is an 'inference' from the conviction that the *Messiah* had suffered the crucifixion, confirmed by the early church's faith that the spiritual presence of the Living Christ was among them. It is true that the New Testament often puts the resurrection in grossly literal and historical terms, though never with the consistency and lack of ambiguity which marks the modern literalist. But the resurrection can never properly in Christianity be conceived as simple history. If so, the doctrine of the 'hiddenness' of God *(Deus absconditus)* is threatened. You will recognize that the problem is classically expressed in Dostoevsky's Grand Inquisitor. 'Sheer' miracle endangers the biblical God and human freedom; it is the invention of the modern (Greek or scholastic) mind. Once again, the historian must dismiss it (the resurrection) as—transhistorical. By reason of methodological limitation, he cannot deal with Creation or Eschaton. They are in the realm of historical mythos (not legend), not historiography."

.   .   .

The Catholic reception of my book was mixed. The greater part of the material in it came out first as a magazine article, and when it appeared, I received a letter—intelligent, polite and appreciative —from Father Frederick L. Moriarty, S.J., of the Jesuit seminary at Weston, Massachusetts. Later, when the book was out, I was sent a copy of the Catholic weekly *America*, which contained a review of it by Father Moriarty, in the same tone and sense as his letter. That issue of *America* (February 4th, 1956) contained, however, a special article by Monsignor John J. Dougherty, professor of Sacred Scripture at the Immaculate Conception Seminary of Darlington, New Jersey, which was designed to put its readers on their guard against me. The methods of Monsignor Dougherty afforded a striking contrast with those of Father Moriarty. "He has taken," said Monsignor Dougherty of me, "*one* hypothetical interpretation, that of the French scholar André Dupont-Sommer of the Sorbonne and presented it, dressed up in exciting diction, to the circle of those who can read and not evaluate. That is mischief. Dupont-Sommer's sensational and unproved thesis, adopted by Wilson, was that the Qumrân documents revealed an anticipation of Christianity in the sect of the Essenes." He then went on to make the point that M. Dupont-Sommer had supported his theory—which involves an assumption that the Teacher of Righteousness anticipated the martyrdom of Jesus—by reading certain words that would favour it into one of the hiatuses of the Habakkuk Commentary. I had myself called attention to this and described it as "a somewhat high-handed conjecture," and it may very well be that Monsignor Dougherty first learned of this point from my book; but he wrote of it in such a way as to suggest that it was something very damaging which I had either not known or suppressed and which he himself was bringing to light to disabuse my ignorant readers. "True," he adds, "in his later work he [Dupont-Sommer] abandoned this and much of his theory, but Mr. Wilson has written just one article, which gives unmerited life to a hypothesis already discarded by its author." This statement is entirely untrue. "The reader will judge for himself," says Dupont-Sommer in the preface to his second book on the scrolls, "how far the views which I put forward in the *Dead Sea Scrolls* have been confirmed or refuted by the new facts. . . . I have tried to the best of my ability to profit from this enormous collective effort [the scholarly studies of the scrolls], and have fairly and objectively examined the new suggestions and criticisms which have been sent to me. Nonetheless, I have not felt that my original opinions have been disproved on

૭ 17 ૭

any fundamental point." It may be added that the audacious conjecture as to the martyrdom of the Teacher of Righteousness has been given a certain support by passages in a Nahum Commentary —recently pieced together and deciphered—that supplements the one on Habakkuk. Monsignor Dougherty, then, has resorted to some dubious devices in order to make an impression on that "circle of those who can read but not evaluate"—that public who knows nothing whatever about what is involved in the controversy— whom he says I am out to hoodwink.

What we have here, then, side by side in a single issue of *America,* are two levels of the Catholic Church : the sophisticated well-educated priest who is speaking to an audience on his own level, without being overheard or misunderstood by the vulgar, and the priest who makes use of trickery to impress his more humble parishioners and to keep them from asking questions. I imagine, in fact, that the Dougherty article was ordered and printed in the same issue to offset the Moriarty review.

．　　　．　　　．

The Catholics have developed, in the modern world—as the Protestants have had to do—a good deal of flexibility; but it works in a different way. A man like Frank Cross or Paul Tillich can simply restate, re-interpret, traditional theological views. The Catholic has to hit upon some gimmick which will enable him to give the impression of eating his cake and having it, too. In my intercourse with the scholarly world in connection with the Dead Sea scrolls, I came upon some curious examples of this. There exists, it seems, a book by a Catholic priest that throws a good deal of new light on the dual authorship of Isaiah; but the Church still maintains that this book was all written by one person, so the author has provided a preface explaining—in blank contradiction to what he has been at pains to show—that his findings have proved the opposite. Another Catholic priest, I am told, has written a biography of Luther in which the leader of the Reformation is presented as a towering religious genius. He gets over the obvious difficulty by contending that what Luther was fighting was not really Catholicism.

．　　　．　　　．

The Catholic, then, does not have to be honest in the sense in which the term is ordinarily used—any more than the Communist does. He deals with the fool according to his folly; he defends the high faith he professes by bringing it down within the range of the low; he is free to think whatever he pleases if he makes a routine submission. The Protestant pastor, on the other hand, must at least make pretensions to honesty as well as to other virtues, because—since the personal conscience is the compass by which Protestants steer—the pastor must set an example, he must illustrate his morality in public; and this is liable to result in hypocrisy—the Protestant failing *par excellence*. We find in the literature of England dozens of whited sepulchres, from Zeal-of-the-Land Busy to Chadband, for the exceptional Tartuffe of Molière. There are in French any number of sinful or corrupted or cruel priests, but the rôle of the priest is different from that of the Protestant minister and the kind of example he sets. The priest proves himself in a different way—he may function by foul means as well as by fair, his temptations are taken for granted; his problems of morality are different. Since he does not make the Protestant's claims to a righteousness, an austerity of life, a devotion to moral principle superior to other men's, he can hardly be a rank or a hollow fraud in the way that the Protestant can.

· · ·

I am glad that I do not myself have to worry about either of these problems : living up to the Protestant virtues or complying with the exactions of the Catholic Church. I even congratulate myself that I do not feel the obligation to adapt my ideas to the formulas—accepted in however symbolical, in however rationalized a form—of traditional Christian theology.

II

The United States

THE UNITED STATES is not a nation in the sense that England or France is. It is a society, a political system, which is still in a somewhat experimental state. Hence our panics of various kinds. One series of these has been due to the fear of subversion by foreign powers. The first of them occurred at the beginning of the Republic, when the menace was the France of the Directory and the Napoleonic era, and the Alien and Sedition Acts were passed. In the middle of the nineteenth century, the Know Nothing movement was stimulated by the great immigrations of Irish and Germans that had followed the blight of the potato famine and the failure of the revolution of 1848. The arrival of all these Catholics raised a bogy of domination by the alien Catholic Church. At the end of the First World War, terrified by the Bolshevik Revolution, we had the first spasm of "Red" hysteria, with its indiscriminate jailings and its illegal wholesale deportations; and at the end of the second war, in our terror of Soviet espionage and Soviet infiltration of the government, this was revived in the MacCarthyan purges. There have, also, been panics of another kind. In the great field for industrial enterprise that the newly opened country provided, the spirit of speculation was likely to rage unrestrained, and this gave rise to gigantic bankruptcies and the breakdown of the money market. As a result of these periodical crises, it was necessary to set up devices for curbing the swindles of the speculators as well as checking the growth of the monopolies which had been choking their lesser competitors, and for providing new land and work for the many who had been ruined by both groups. What has always been at stake in these crises is the political system itself. The country has tended to oscillate between phases when the big money interests are plundering the rest of the people and phases when the problem is faced of making the actualities of American life approximate to the principles laid down by the Declaration of Independence. There is a basic contradiction and difficulty here which the founders could hardly have foreseen. The reformers of the eighteenth century liked to formulate the ideal at which they were aiming as "the career open to the talents." They wanted to establish a society in which everyone, to the extent of his abilities, would be given an equal chance, and a Condorcet or a Jefferson imagined a state of things in which people like themselves, from whatever stratum, would be free to get an education, to hold office, to work for the common good. They could not imagine that a race would arise who would exploit the opportunities of freedom, at the expense of the common good, simply to enrich themselves. The aptitude for cashing-in was a talent—to which, along with the others, the career was now perfectly open—that had not been taken into account by a Jefferson; and the result of the whole situation was that you had, on the one hand, the millionaire insisting on his right to freedom to do as well for himself as he could, and, on the other, the unfortunate citizen—squeezed out by the rich man's monopoly, left penniless by the failure of his banks, compelled to work in his factories or reduced to a bare subsistence by his money-lending tricks and the prices he charged for the necessaries of life —complaining that conditions in the United States were depriving him of the national right to life, liberty and the pursuit of happiness. Since both sides are claiming this right, these crises have to be met with compromise.

There has been also the crisis of the Civil War, when the Union itself was in danger. The Republic has thus had to be saved over and over again, and it continues to have to be saved. This has not been the case over so long a period with any European country of either the monarchic or the republican kind—and the situation with us has always been, in some ways, so different from any European one that happenings in the United States are hardly comprehensible to Europeans. They could see, for example, during the New Deal, that Franklin D. Roosevelt was attacking the crisis with a bold and a free hand, but they could not understand how cardinal his rôle as an American president was, and that this cardinal rôle recurs.

.   .   .

Our presidents have run in sequences, and since the middle of the nineteenth century, they have tended to be classifiable under three main types. You have, first, the public-spirited idealist who may or may not be a good politician, but who knows American history, understands the importance and the meaning of the United States in the larger world and assumes the responsibility of maintaining our unique rôle. The first seven American presidents necessarily belonged to this type, and we have had several men of this calibre since, though only at irregular intervals: Lincoln, Theodore Roosevelt, Woodrow Wilson, Franklin Roosevelt. All four of these gave everything they had—Lincoln, Wilson and Franklin Roosevelt their lives—worthily to represent the United States of America, to preside over, direct and take part in the next act of the republican drama. An administration on this high level is likely, however, to be followed by a slump, with an inferior type of man in office : the small party politician—the Warren G. Harding or Harry S. Truman. This type has but little conception of what the other kind of president has been up to. He is a product of his party machine, in which he has had his whole existence and which circumscribes his whole ambition. It has been for him not only his profession, but also his college, his church and his club; it has even become somehow his country. He puts old party pals in office, and when, as invariably happens—Teapot Dome, the Pauley appointment, General Vaughn and his colleagues—the latter get into trouble for trafficking in public property or taking presents from industrial interests, the president of this stripe has no thought except to protect them. For him, party loyalty is everything. Virtue, in the school he has been to, means constancy in sticking by one's team-mates, and it is doubtful whether President Truman ever really understood, in Pauley's case, what people were complaining about when they objected that a lobbyist for the oil companies ought not to be made Undersecretary of the Navy. A president of this kind inhabits so different a world from the man of high civic conscience that the outlook and the language of the latter are hardly intelligible to him, and Truman, succeeding Roosevelt, would be touching in his failure to connect with his chief if he had not preserved all the smugness of the sound and successful party man. A third type, clearly defined, is the man who neither knows about professional politics nor understands the problems of government, but has arrived at a position of eminence through achievement in some quite different field : Grant, Hoover, Eisenhower. These three—two generals and an engineer—were put in by the Republican interests for the reason that they combined being popular heroes whom the public could be made to accept with an ignorance both of politics and of economics. They can be depended upon not to obstruct the designs of big business, and one of the features of their administrations is the extreme naïveté they are likely to show in inviting big business to take possession. Grant nominated as his Secretary of the Treasury Alexander Stewart, a drygoods millionaire, and was surprised to learn of the law which debarred this office to merchants. In the same way, President Eisenhower selected as Secretary of Defence Charles E. Wilson, the president of General Motors, and was equally surprised to learn that a man with large industrial interests was not eligible for this post. This was also, it would seem, news to Wilson, who announced that no alarm need be felt, since "for years" he had "thought that what was good for our country was good for General Motors and vice versa"; but he was obliged to go through the forms of getting rid of his General Motors stock. There is, also, perhaps, a fourth category of presidents which stands out less sharply than the other three : the kind of "borderline case" represented by Grover Cleveland and William Howard Taft. Such men stand also for the *status quo,* but they bring to public office special qualities of training and integrity.

.   .   .

A discussion of the various types of presidents suggests an important distinction that runs all through American life. This distinction has little in common with any to be found in Europe, since it does not depend on rank or class. To simplify, one can say that, on the one hand, you find in the United States the people who are constantly aware—as is the first type of president above—that, beyond their opportunities for money-making, they have a stake in the success of our system, that they share the responsibility to carry on its institutions, to find expression for its new point of view, to give it dignity, to make it work; and, on the other hand, the people who are merely concerned with making a living or a fortune, with practising some profession or mastering some technical skill, as they would in any other country, and who lack, or do not possess to quite the same degree the sense of America's rôle. This difference was so marked in my youth—it has probably become less so now—that even in that period of the early nineteen hundreds, overpowered though it partly was by the atmosphere of millionaires' mansions and luxurious country clubs, the children of serious republicans (of course, with a small *r*) in any of the old universities, could be recognized—*rari nantes*—among the debonair young men who were planning to be bond salesmen and brokers, as almost belonging to a different race. This was not merely a matter of education or of coming from the Eastern seaboard : the Middle Western countryman Lincoln had this sense as highly developed as any New Englander from Harvard. Nor was it a matter of blood—Anglo-Saxon or Dutch—or of ancestry—a family from the seventeenth century : Jacob Riis and Carl Schurz had it as much as Theodore Roosevelt or of any of the Adamses or Lodges.

Before the Civil War, this republican patriotism was shared by the North and the South; and those Southerners who relied upon or were carrying on the American political tradition of Jefferson and the other Virginian statesmen were terribly perplexed and torn when the conceptions on which they had been living began to be broken down. Calhoun is the great example. The war, in disrupting the states, prevented the South thereafter from ever in quite the same way as in the years of the Revolution making common cause with the North. Yet a Northerner imbued with this sense will feel far more in common with a Southerner who has derived the same instinct from his background—whatever may be their other differences—than with a Northerner who has not. A curious

affirmation of this spirit in the teeth of the Civil War is described
or imagined by Harold Frederic, the novelist of northern New York
State, in his story *The Copperhead*. Opinion in upstate New York
did not always go along with New England, and there was a good
deal of disaffection at the time of the war. An anti-Unionist paper
was published in Watertown, and Horatio Seymour of Onondaga
County, the Governor of New York City, was suspected of having
connived at the riots against the draft. In *The Copperhead,* an upstate farmer, possessed by the tradition of the Revolution—the only
books he has read are histories of the Revolution—runs head-on
against public opinion by championing the right of the South to
secede. Local feeling—as the war continues and the other farmers
lose their sons—becomes more and more bitter against him. His
own son in time enlists, and the father is struck speechless with
indignation. The neighbours become so incensed that they set out
to tar and feather him, but when he comes to the door and defies
them, they cannot face him and set fire to his house. And at last
he extorts their respect. Obscurely, they recognize, when the war is
over, that by a course of conduct opposed to theirs, by refusing to
take any part in the coercion of the seceding Southerners, he has
been true to his own ideal of American republican freedom. They
make to him their sober apologies and raise money to build him a
new house.

I do not mean to exalt this republican sense as the touchstone
of American merit. A good many of our distinguished men have
had it to a greater or less degree, but some have not had it at all.
Justice Holmes felt a stake in the United States of a kind that his
friend Henry James did not feel. He had served for three years
in the Civil War; and he spent all the rest of his life grinding out
judicial decisions on the benches of the Supreme Courts of
Massachusetts and of the United States. A good deal that went on
in the United States after the Civil War was certainly distasteful
to him; he was even disposed to question the ideals of democratic
government that the Republic was supposed to embody. Yet
Holmes's whole life as a judge was as much in the service of the
United States as his soldiering in the Army of the Potomac. In his
attitude towards Henry and William James, he does show a certain
condescension of the Bostonian of Puritan stock towards the more

recently Americanized Irish. But this is not really the point. Many a New Englander of the sacred breed has shown far less sympathy with the United States, and less responsibility towards it, than William and Henry James. The point I am making here is that a difference does exist between Justice Holmes, on the one hand, and Henry James—if not William—on the other. This difference derives from the fact that Holmes had, as James had not, *identified* his own interests with those of the American Republic. Henry James was much concerned with America, and he felt towards it a certain loyalty, but almost—if not quite to the same degree—in the same nonparticipant way that George Santayana did. The primary stake of James was in the art of imaginative literature, which was for him international, as the stake of Santayana was in the practice of a philosophic criticism that had to be supernational. As for Whistler, who had been to West Point but did not "choose to have been born in Lawrence, Mass.," he does not, in his truculence towards the English, ever seem to have been aware of any rankling of the spirit of seventy-six. His father, George Washington Whistler, who built the Petersburg-Moscow railroad and died in St. Petersburg, had already, as an engineer, arrived at internationality.

I do not, therefore, mean to imply that it is necessarily more desirable, from the point of view of human achievement, to be Lincoln or Justice Holmes or either of the Roosevelts than to be Henry James or Santayana or any of the technical experts who may do their best work abroad—or, for that matter, here at home —without worrying about the Republic. I simply want to show this distinction and to suggest that it ought to be borne in mind. It may, for the foreigner, provide a key to some of the conspicuous paradoxes that seem puzzling in American life.

.   .   .

It is a mistake for the United States to pretend, as we sometimes do, that we have never aimed at "territorial aggrandizement" or encroached on the property of our neighbours. There are people who do believe this, but anyone who has read our history knows that it is not true, and that our acts of intervention and aggression have invariably provoked bitter protests from Americans who believed in our declared ideal. The fact, of course, is that the

United States—like any other expanding political organism—has taken what was useful to it by such means as came to hand. If we could not obtain what we wanted by peaceful negotiation—as we did the Oregon Territory from the English—we have not hesitated to use armed force. Texas was wrested from Mexico by colonists from the United States, and afterwards annexed to the Union. California was acquired through a war with the Mexicans that many people thought high-handed and contrary to the national principles—including both Lincoln and Grant. But Lincoln, then a young politician, supported it once it was started; and Grant, a young lieutenant, took part in the invasion of Mexico. Later on, by destroying the Spanish fleet at the battle of Santiago and occupying Cuba and Puerto Rico, we forced Spain to give up these islands as well as cede to us Guam and the Philippines—though idealistic literary men such as Mark Twain and William Vaughn Moody denounced the whole affair as a national disgrace; and Panama was detached from Colombia by a trick of Theodore Roosevelt's—the incitement of a revolution which gave him a pretext to seize it—that was worthy of Otto von Bismarck, but is not, as a rule, in the United States, referred to with the same disapproval as the ruse of the Ems Telegram. In the meantime, the federal government had fought with a group of the Southern states a relentless and successful war to prevent them from seceding from the Union and had kept them, after its victory, more or less for eleven years, under military occupation. All these steps, as they were taken, of course, were justified by righteous arraignments and humanitarian motives—Spanish atrocities, bad faith of the Mexicans, the injustices of slavery, and so forth; but not one of these provocations would ever have led to war by a process of mere moral logic. What was behind them was the irresistible impulse to spread out over the whole great belt that spans the continent from Atlantic to Pacific, to secure for ourselves outposts in both oceans, and once we had got all this, to make sure that we did not lose any part of it. The phrase by which we referred to this impulse (coined in 1845) was Manifest Destiny—which, however, was a better way of putting it than the slogan of the White Man's Burden that Kipling attempted to foist on us. It should never be attempted to make out a case for such exploits on moral grounds.

I shall return to this subject in the following section; but, in the meantime, it ought to be recognized that the phenomenon we are dealing with here is common to all social-political units that generate a force of expansion. The United States has not been exempt from the appetites that led to the conquests of Nebuchadnezzar's Nineveh, Caesar's Rome or Bonaparte's France.

Americanism

It is curious to trace the vicissitudes of the term *Americanism*. The first quotation given in the *Dictionary of Americanisms* published by Chicago University is from a letter of Jefferson's of 1797 : "The parties here in debate continually charged each other . . . with being governed by an attachment to this or that of the belligerent nations, rather than the dictates of reason and pure Americanism." This is Americanism in the sense defined by Webster (1906) as "a love of America and preference of her interest." In Jefferson's time, of course, it meant the interests of the revolted colonists. But by the fifties of the following century, the word *Americanism* was to take on a new political meaning. It was used by the American or Know Nothing party to designate its own policy—already mentioned above—of combating the Roman Catholicism of German and Irish immigrants and of debarring persons of foreign birth from exercising political rights till they had lived here twenty-one years. It is in this sense that Lincoln uses it when, in a letter of May 15th, 1858, he speaks of the chances of the Republican party : "I think our prospects gradually, and steadily, grow better; though we are not clear out of the woods by a great deal. There is still some effort to make trouble out of 'Americanism.' " This meaning was soon to lapse with the demise of the Know Nothing party. But the word was to be revived, with quite different implications, by Theodore Roosevelt in the nineties. The first use of it in Roosevelt's correspondence is in a letter of December 8th, 1888, to Thomas R. Lounsbury, congratulating him on his *Life of Cooper:* "As a very sincere American myself, I feel like thanking you for the genuine Americanism of your book; which is quite as much displayed in its criticisms as in its praises." Here he is speaking merely of an American point of view; but by the time he writes to William Archer in 1899 (August 31st), he is giving the word a meaning of his own : "I have exactly the feeling about Americanism you describe. Most important of all is it for this country to treat an American on his worth as a man, and to disregard absolutely whether he be of English, German, Irish or any other nation; whether he be of Catholic or Protestant faith." . . . This is Roosevelt at his best. He has changed the Know Nothings' emphasis : instead of wanting to exclude the immigrant, he wishes to take him in and to propose a common ideal of disinterested public service. He is to talk, from the nineties on, a good deal about Americanism, and to give the word a general currency. He is eventually to make it stand for the whole of his political philosophy. Here is his definition in a letter to S. Stanwood Menken of January 10th, 1917 : "Americanism means many things. It means equality of rights and therefore equality of duty and of obligation. It means service to our common country. It means loyalty to one flag, to our flag, the flag of all of us. It means on the part of each of us respect for the rights of the rest of us. It means that all of us guarantee the rights of each of us. It means free education, genuinely representative government, freedom of speech and thought, equality before the law for all men, genuine political and religious freedom, and the democratizing of industry so as to give at least a measurable quality of opportunity for all, and so as to place before us, as our ideal in all industries where this ideal is possible of attainment, the system of co-operative ownership and management, in order that the tool-users may, so far as possible, become the tool-owners. Everything is un-American that tends either to government by a plutocracy or government by a mob. To divide along the lines of section or caste or creed is un-American. All privileges based on wealth, and all enmity to honest men merely because they are wealthy, are un-American—both of them equally so. Americanism means the virtues of courage, honour, justice, truth, sincerity, and hardihood—the virtues that made America." The last letter included in his published correspondence—written on January 3rd, 1919, three days before his death, to be read at a benefit concert of the American Defense Society—has, however, an emphasis that is somewhat different. This was written at the end of the first world war, in the era—referred to above—of the mass deportation of radicals. The old chief in retirement had by this time passed into an apoplectic phase in which he was convinced, for example, that the International Workers of the World were necessarily a criminal organization and that labour leaders were guilty, as a matter of course, of the crimes of which, in that moment of hysteria, they were lavishly being accused. "There must be no sagging back," writes Roosevelt, "in the fight for Americanism merely because the war is over. . . . There can be no divided allegiance here. . . . Any man who says he is an American, but something else also, isn't an American at all. We have room for but one flag, the American flag, and this excludes the red flag which symbolizes all wars against liberty and civilization just as much as it excludes any foreign flag of a nation to which we are hostile." This is the fear of the foreigner again. It was rampant after Roosevelt's death, and anyone with a non-Anglo-Saxon name who ventured to complain about anything or to propose a social reform was likely to be told at once that if he didn't like it here in the United States, he ought to go back where he came from. By this time, the very term "Americanism" had become a blackmailing menace. One remembers reading in the New York *Tribune* of March 3rd, 1920, that the younger Theodore Roosevelt, chairman of the American Legion's "Americanism Commission," had called a meeting "at which it was decided to thoroughly Americanize all war veterans, then to utilize them in the work of making good citizens of the foreign-born of the State." It may not be true that "Americanism"—like Dr. Johnson's "patriotism"—is invariably "the last refuge of a scoundrel"; but it has been made to serve some very bad causes, and is now a word to avoid.

III

War

THE QUESTION of American expansion brings us to the subject of war. Why *do* human beings go to war. At one time, I was somewhat impressed by the Marxist explanation of this : economic rivalries for markets and the need for fresh fields of exploitation. Now, it is true that economic interests are usually involved in wars, but does this really account for what happens? Is it true, for example, that the United States took part in the last two wars with Germany for the reason that the Kaiser and Hitler were threatening our economic future or because—another of the Marxist motivations—Woodrow Wilson and Franklin Roosevelt resorted to war production and military service to get themselves out of their capitalist quandaries of unemployment and commercial deflation? Add to these explanations the fact that certain elements in the United States are pushovers for British propaganda, and that the Germans have made it so difficult to maintain a neutrality towards them that one is sometimes tempted to imagine that, once Germany is launched on a war, she at once sets up herself a bureau of anti-German propaganda, designed to provoke other countries to come into the conflict against her. Yet all this, it seems to me, still, does not entirely account for the rôle of the United States in the last two European wars.

.   .   .

I was personally, in the case of both wars, opposed to our becoming involved in them. I was nineteen at the beginning of the first one, and I happened to be in London in August of 1914. The declaration of war against Germany came on a bank holiday, and the holiday—on account of the crisis—was prolonged for a day or so. What astonished me was the popular enthusiasm : people riding on top of taxis, cheering in the crowded streets; a mob around Buckingham Palace calling for the King and Queen—"Mary! we're wyting !"—making them come back to the balcony over and over again : a silly and undignified performance; singers in the music halls reviving the banal old Boer War song *Soldiers of the Queen* ("When we have to show them what we mean !"). I wondered whether they thought that the war was all going to be a tremendous bank holiday. When I got back to the United States, I read—in 1916—a book by Mr. Leonard Woolf, with a preface by Bernard Shaw—a book called *International Government,* in which he showed that international business and the international labour movement would soon put an end to wars, which, from the point of view of the interests of either of these powerful groups, had nothing to recommend them. I was convinced by the arguments of Woolf, and I heartily approved of Wilson when he said there was such a thing as a nation's being too proud to fight, as later I approved of Charles Beard when he insisted, at the beginning of the second war, that we had better let Europe alone and set our own house in order. The Germany of Hitler, to be sure, seemed more threatening than that of the Kaiser; but I believed that there would have been no Hitler if there had been no Treaty of Versailles, and that the stalemate to which the Allies and the Central Powers would certainly have been brought if we had not intervened would have averted so disastrous a settlement, and I now doubted whether any liberties which Europe herself could not defend were worth their cost in American lives. So I remained still an isolationist, unmoved by the pleas of the British.

I was a regular reader during the first of these wars of an excellent American liberal weekly—founded in 1914; and in the twenties I began to write for it and eventually became one of its editors. In the early days of the war, this paper had been quite close to the White House and had supported the peace policy of Wilson. I was therefore rather taken aback when, after getting himself re-elected on the basis of having "kept us out of war," he proceeded to lead

us in, and was followed by this liberal weekly, which insisted, however, as Wilson did, that the American objective was peace with
justice and the world made safe for democracy. One of the editors
of this magazine was supposed to have collaborated with Wilson in
framing the Fourteen Points. But from the moment, at the end of
the war, that the results were before its editors, they were obliged
to repudiate the Treaty of Versailles, to expose its betrayal of our
aims and its ultimate impracticability. Years afterwards, when I
worked on this paper, I once had a conversation with its editor-
in-chief, for whom I had much respect, on the subject of his policy
at the time of the war. He surprised and rather shocked me by
justifying his former support of American intervention in Europe
on the ground that not to have taken part would have been "so
second rate." This argument did not seem to me serious, and I
ascribed it to his own British origins. Both his parents—though his
mother was Irish—had been born on the other side, and I had
noted that, helpful to labour though our policy was supposed to
be, he had winced with as much embarrassment at the lower-class
manners and accents of visiting British labour men as if he had
been born there himself.

When our editor-in-chief died, the paper was run by a group
composed of the other editors. The weekly had been handsomely
subsidized, first by an idealistic millionaire, then, after his death,
by his widow—both personal friends of the editor. But this lady
now married an Englishman, went permanently to live in England
and became a British subject. She had, however, arranged, in New
York, a foundation which was to function in her absence, automatically supplying such money as was needed to make up our
deficits; and we were given to understand that we were just as free
as our late chief had been to publish whatever we pleased. This
went well until the second war with Germany, in regard to which
the paper's policy was completely isolationist. In the autumn of
1940, the husband of our Anglicized patroness suddenly descended
on us, and indignantly denounced this policy. He particularly
pointed to a passage in one of our editorial paragraphs in which
the writer had made some reference to "the struggle of imperialisms
in the Balkans." One of these imperialisms was England, and this
Britisher made it clear that his country was not so to be character-

ized. He dissolved the old staff of the paper, though the members —to diminish the scandal—were allowed still to haunt the office and to continue in a small way to write till they were able to find other work. The managing editor was kept, at the price of his reversing his position and writing strongly interventionist leaders instead of isolationist ones. Our English patron-in-law took over the direction of the paper and published anonymous leaders, entirely composed by himself, which would have been intensely comic if the situation had not been humiliating—since they purported to express the opinions of the well-known American editors but were actually exclusively occupied with plugging, in British clichés, the official British point of view. A stop had been put at once to our criticisms of the Roosevelt administration, and a regular political commentator who had frequently disagreed with its policies was summarily dismissed. It was proposed, in an issue of December 1940, that "the United States and Great Britain assume responsibility and leadership for the whole world, except for that part of it at present under the heel of the totalitarians. Let these two great repositories of democracy pool their leadership in brains, vision and courage. . . . It is clear that we should extend the utmost aid to Great Britain even if it involves a considerable danger of going to war." And the American readers were plied with the reasonings of disinterested candour: "Would the nations in the British Commonwealth play fair in such a plan? No final guarantee can be given, but we feel the chance is an excellent one that they would. . . . Would the Americans play fair? One can no more give guarantees for this than one can for their British Commonwealth cousins." Our new director and cousin did not, however, take account of the shock to the regular readers of the paper, who saw it turn its coat overnight and knew there was something wrong. From that moment, it lost credit with its public, and it has never recovered since.

But the United States went in on the British side, and the collapse of our liberal weekly, as well as the impotence of once influential persons like Charles Beard and Stuart Chase to command any kind of hearing when they urged us to stay out of Europe, forced me to take account, in a way that I had not done before, of the inveterate and irrational instinct that impels human beings to go to war. In the second of these battering-matches, the soldiers did not find themselves crawling around in the mud and the lice of the trenches, which had made the conditions of the first world war peculiarly dismal and gruesome : they were flying about in the air with a certain exhilaration, and this gave the whole thing a zoological aspect that had not so much struck me in the earlier war. There was here a kind of free-for-all among the wasps and the bees, and this made the previous conflict look, in retrospect, like a battle of ants. Once one of these mêlées was started— though thousands of miles away, in a continent we had left behind —we would watch it for a time with great interest, then be stirred by an overwhelming impulse to get into it and show our mettle. The middle-aged newspaper-reader sat at home with a certain complacency, looking on while the Germans and Russians were buzzing out at one another, unaware that our high-flying American insects were itching to buzz out, too; that the Japanese insects were itching, and that these would soon give us a pretext for taking part in the general field day.

The official propaganda for war had been relatively inexpert in 1917. When the ex-soldiers came to write books, these showed not a trace of its influence save to dismiss all its slogans as swindles. But the sales talk of our government for the second one was a smooth and professional job, and though a few of our ex-service writers had never swallowed it or had spewed it up, a good many of them accepted its formulas and made them the basis of their work. That once useful phrase "Manifest Destiny" had by this time become old-fashioned, and the idea was now restated in terms of the superiority of our American civilization over others. The word *Americanism* which, as I have shown, after Theodore Roosevelt, had degenerated into pure cant, was discarded in favour of the less metaphysical "American Way of Life." This sounded as if we had in America something guaranteed to give satisfaction, and its commercial associations, if not its commercial origin, are indicated by the only quotation—of 1914—in the *Dictionary of Americanisms:* "This is dangerous ground, as Professor Hutchins well knows, and it strikes at the very heart of what the business magazines like to call 'The American Way of Life'!" The American missionaries of our way of life, the European defenders of "the free world" and the Soviet installers of the "people's democracies" all found themselves united against Hitler, the three powers having in common—not surely their democratic institutions—but simply their common fear; and they were soon, as they began to defeat him, wrecking the German cities and raping the German women just as the Germans had done with their own, and spitting on the civilization they claimed to be fighting for by bombing—for no military advantage—the house of Goethe at Frankfurt along with its other ancient monuments (while its industries were left almost untouched), and the theatres and galleries of Munich; and finally —a feat that the United States, with its formidable technical development, was wonderfully equipped to accomplish—wiping out a whole Japanese city with a marvellous new kind of explosive. In producing these city-annihilating bombs, the Russians—once the menace of Hitler was removed—were soon hastening to emulate us, and we have both gone on to explosives even more devastating, till men are now able to boast that they have finally been able to devise, in their strife against one another, weapons that are capable not only of exterminating the whole human race but of putting an end to life on this planet. Now, what is the explanation of this : a paradox grotesque but all-threatening, inconceivable yet weighing on our lives?

It is easy to say that war is nowadays a mere bad habit inherited from a barbaric past, when peoples were so isolated from one another, so impeded by their different languages from arriving at an understanding, as well as so much under the compulsion of the appetite for predatory exploits, that it was natural for them to fight things out. But we ought to try to get behind this, to try to grasp what this habit consists of, what it implies about human behaviour; and in order to arrive at that, we must learn to approach human life from a point of view more zoological than is usual for either editorial writers or for serious professional philosophers. It is true, as I have said above, that we have lately been coming to recognize that those animals we characterize as "lower" have a good deal more in common with us than, in the first chill of newly found cousinship, we formerly cared to admit. But we still do not recognize sufficiently how much of what we do and are is not penetrated, is not even scrutinized, by the faculty we call our "reason," how much is determined by processes as much hidden from us as those which have produced our organs, processes we can fathom so little with our conscious and "reasoning" minds that we still, in certain philosophic quarters, fall back, in connection with them, on the vague conception of "God." The absurdity on the part of nations at war of invoking, on both sides, this "God" is due really to the fact that the impulse to fight is something so strong, so deep-seated, so uncontrollable by—one might almost say, so unaccountable to—reason, something to which it is so difficult still to oppose a successful resistance, that the only justification we can find for it is the same as our way of accounting for the incredible ingenuity of our physiological systems. We are at least a little beginning to get the hang of how these systems operate. Anatomy is already an old story; the functions of the brain are being explored; we know something of how sex is determined and how family characteristics are inherited. We have come to know a little, since Freud, about the factors that influence people in those preferences of sexual selection that go by the name of "love." We know something, through Marx and Engels, of the frequently unavowed, if not always unconscious, stimuli of a social-economic kind that play their part in provoking the modern wars. Yet the group behaviour of insects enables us to study our own and to draw conclusions about it that the logic of Marx and Engels —as well as their German idealism—would not allow them to take into account. It would seem that the higher we go in the scale of animal types, the more elaborately is the brain developed, and hence the more important in the life of the group does the individual unit become. Since we find ourselves, we human beings, at the furthest point of this development, we can hardly imagine the experience of the less cerebral forms of life. At first, as I have said above, we ascribed to them something called "blind instinct," which motivated all that they did. More recently we have come to see certain of their acts as determined by some such activity as we mean, in connection with human beings, by "thinking things out for themselves." Yet behind this we cannot imagine what happens : we can only see from how they behave that they are animated by a kind of group consciousness, that they operate by a kind of group brain. How are the habits, the skills, the knowledge that have been stored in this brain transmitted? Where are they accumulated? The bees communicate through code; but how do the migrant birds —from generation to generation—communicate their memory of airways? Do the younger birds learn from the old in accompanying them on their travels? Then what about that flock of butterflies, also in course of migration, who are reported to have circled in bewilderment over the spot, on a street in New Jersey, where their species, in previous years, had had the habit of stopping off? These butterflies could bring with them no experienced guides : they were a new generation every season. Had they inherited the memory of the tree with their genes? In any case, in knowing its location and expecting to find it useful, they would not seem as individuals to have been exercising what we call judgment. And how do the ants and the termites succeed in doing what they do? —making bridges over dangerous rivers, forming ranks for well-organized wars. It seems to us that our own operations are planned, directed and carried out in a way that is not possible for insects; yet we Japanese and Germans and Americans are obviously doing on a bigger scale the same sort of thing as they. Are not our enterprises—of war, expansion, domination, adventure, consolidation— far more the results of group impulse than we imagine when the moves of some other group leads first to diplomatic protests than to a formal declaration of war? Are they not something very primitive, so far beyond the reach of our judgment that we are not even aware of their nature? The objectives we announce for the sake of form turn out to have little relation to what we actually do if we win. The ants simply eat their enemies, and there is always an element of this in the outcome of any war.

Confession of a Non-Fighter

In the first of the two world wars, I spent almost two years in the Army—a year and a half of that time in France—first, as a private in the hospital corps at a base hospital in the Vosges; and afterwards as a sergeant in the intelligence service at the American headquarters in Chaumont. A summer at the Plattsburg training camp, before we entered the war, had convinced me I was incapable of becoming an officer and that, in general, I loathed the Army. I could not imagine commanding men, and I could not imagine killing them—at least, men I did not know, and in cold blood. In the second war—by that time I was fifty—I went abroad as a correspondent, and visited England, Italy and Greece. Although, as I say above, I was anything but enthusiastic about our entering the first of these wars, I did not—just out of college, and with all my friends in the service—take a stand against serving in it, but I enlisted in the hospital unit in order not to wait for the draft and because it would not involve fighting. Later on—once a part of the Army, and under pressure of the wartime atmosphere —I made some probably rather insincere gestures in the direction of getting myself transferred to some more active branch of the service; but I have never, in later life, regretted for a moment that I have been able to get through both of these horrible affairs without killing or wounding anybody and without getting killed or wounded; that I made no serious sacrifices for either of them— causes in which I did not believe—and have survived to occupy myself with something in which I do believe : literature. I have been fortunate, besides, in both my wars, for, in the course of them, I saw a good deal of the world and aspects of human life that I would hardly have come up against otherwise.

IV

Europe

I HAD THOUGHT I should be glad to see France in February 1954, when I arrived at Calais from England, but, looking out the window of the boat-train in the late winter afternoon, I was seized by a sharp irritation. It was cold in the car, and the weather was dismal : a damp mist over greying snow. This landscape—such a waste in itself—was littered with the wreckage of bombings, which reminded me of the wreckage of Italy in the summer of 1945. Nine years later, in France, these buildings had not been rebuilt nor the rubbish even cleared away. It reminded me, also, of the winter of 1917, when, a soldier in the American Expeditionary Force, I had made the long journey from Le Hâvre to Vittel in a crowded and unheated box-car through a similarly dismal countryside similarly damp with mist. Later on, I had flopped with my company on narrow army cots in a palatial and freezing chamber, where our breaths went up as steam. This room was the salle of the Casino at Vittel, the fashionable summer resort in the Vosges where my hospital unit was stationed, and when one came to in the morning in the chilly air, to the curses and obscene shouts of one's equally uncomfortable companions, one looked up at the high painted ceiling full of the muses and floating goddesses held appropriate to such places in Europe. This casino I was later to remember when, in 1954, I came to lodge at Salzburg in the Leopoldskron, where I was one of the visiting lecturers in the American Seminar, a curious kind of school intended to impart some knowledge of American institutions and

culture to interested students in Europe. The seventeenth century
castle was almost as cold as the Casino in Vittel. It was also at
least equally fancy; and, just as in the Vosges I had struggled with
a stifling bronchitis of my own as well as the diseases of our
patients, so here, at nine in the morning, I lectured, with a bad
throat that continually set me coughing and with red and rheumy
eyes—a conjunctivitis that went, I was told, in classical combination with the bronchial and digestive disorders from which I was
also suffering—among glass and porcelain chandeliers, proctic
cupids and painted panels, stucco ornaments like Viennese pastry
and portraits of Austrian ecclesiastics who had the look of insipid
old ladies, while, outside, the familiar snow that thawed as soon
as it fell was exhaling in the same damp mist. In 1917 we had
been saving Europe from the Germans; in the forties we had been
saving it from the Germans again; we shall presently be returning
no doubt—unless our mentality changes—to rescue it from the
Russians. But the more we save Europe from the Huns and the
Goths, the more wretched she seems to get. Was she really proud
and splendid in our youth? How demoralized France became at
the end of the first of these wars; how depraved and macabre the
whole continent at the end of the second one; how far gone in
decomposition seem so many things one sees there today! How
futile to try to save Europe, who does nothing to save herself!

.   .   .

One of the most discouraging symptoms, for the American
visitor in Europe, is the recent multiplication of languages. You
have now the revival of Gaelic as a nationalistic gesture in Scot-
land as well as its installation as the official language of Ireland,
and the nursing as a literary language of the local Norwegian
dialect called *landsmoll* in place of Dano-Norwegian, the language
in which Ibsen wrote. I learned at the Salzburg Seminar from
Jugoslav students that Jugoslavia maintains four languages—
Serbian, Croatian, Slovenian and Macedonian—at least three of
which seemed to have literatures; and I was told that the Swiss,
not content with their German, French and Italian, the second of
these the language of Rousseau, the first of Burckhardt and Keller,
have been cultivating as a literary medium their old Latin folk-

language Romansh and even having taught in their schools the
dialects of the different cantons. To an American, this seems
perfect madness; to a pre-1914 internationalist, a perverse setting-
back of history. As if the differences in language in Europe had
not made enough trouble already! How tired we were in America
of hearing how the French and the Germans could not understand
one another! We could sympathize fully with the struggles of the
Irish and Scottish against the English, of the Hungarians, Poles
and Czechs against their Germanic oppressors; it was natural
enough, to be sure, to resent the oppressor's language, especially
imposed in schools to the exclusion of one's native tongue; but
why cultivate tongues that are dying out or that will only be
learned by the people of a relatively small nationality at the
expense of those of wider currency? Surely Conrad, though his
English sounds foreign, is far more important as an English writer
than he could ever have been in Polish. The Irish have produced
in English magnificent literature. James Joyce and Bernard Shaw
are world figures, who tower above their English-born contempor-
aries; Yeats is one of the great English poets. But how is it possible,
at this late date, to develop a folk-language like Gaelic to the
point where it would be capable of anything of Joycean or Shavian
complexity? It is as much, I am told, as the Irish can do, to equip
it with an invented vocabulary for dealing with the phenomena of
modern life. The revival of Hebrew in Israel has undoubtedly
more justification. There is a need for a common language among
the diversity of Jews—German, East European, Russian, British,
North African and Yemenite; and Hebrew, as a literary medium,
has never been entirely dead. Yet one cannot but regret this necessity. To write even in modernized Hebrew seems to lead back into
a cabinned and visionary past from which the great Jewish
thinkers and writers in the European and Slavic languages have
succeeded in liberating themselves.

It is dismaying, to the non-nationalistic observer from our feder-
ated United States, to find Europe, not only not more unified,
not only not in process of unification, but, on the contrary,
it would appear, more lacking in coherence than ever. He
may reflect, with a certain smugness, that the population of
the United States includes at the present time, large elements

from all the Slavic as well as all the European nationalities, as well as many Negroes and orientals, who sometimes go on speaking their original tongues for two or three generations, and that, in spite of our recurrent anti-alien alarms and a certain amount of friction, we are not being continually torn by nationalistic feuds. We have had one bitter sectional war—between the North and the South; we have still—in the Southern states and sometimes in other places—a very bad situation between the whites and the Negroes. But the lack of cordial relations between, on the one hand, the Americans of Dutch and Anglo-Saxon blood and, on the other, the immigrants of other stocks—though it still plays a part in politics and is sometimes an impediment to social life—hardly figures today as an element that makes for disunity, just as the Dutch and the English themselves, so hostile to one another in the eighteenth century, have now become completely merged. Why on earth, the American asks, have the idiotic Europeans not organized long ago—as we and the Soviet Union have done—in a comprehensive federation? If the Soviets and the States are now powerful, and if Europe seems impotent, collapsed, as the result of suicidal wars, it is because we have this advantage. In Europe, they seem still to think only in old-fashioned terms of hegemony. Napoleon attempted this but overshot the mark in Russia and aroused the apprehensions of the English, who finally put him down. The Germans have tried the same thing, but again aroused the fears of the English, who, although they have not themselves wanted to dominate Europe—having an empire farther off and for the most part easier to handle—have prevented anyone else from doing so. The result has been a stalemate, this wreckage, both the great units stripped of their power, and the Continent, as a whole, left in fragments.

But why, the American demands, this *passion* for fragmentation? In America, we like to have our people get along as well as possible together. Our slogan is "the melting pot." There must exist some strong motivation which is hard for the American to grasp that drives even the tiniest national group both in the British Isles and on the continent to this wrong-headed nationalism. How far this process has gone was lately brought home to me in a striking way by a discussion with a young Irishwoman who had grown up under the Eire régime. I had previously been talking about Ireland with an Irishwoman of a slightly older generation who was closer to the old intellectual Ireland, the Ireland of Yeats and Joyce, of which, through its visitors to the States and some that had settled here, I had had some attractive glimpses. She, too, had grown up in Eire, and she looked back on eleven years of Gaelic as an appalling tract of waste in her life. Since the subject was so limited, she told me, they had eventually to occupy the students by making them memorize the Gaelic vocabulary—itself a synthetic product—for the various diseases of cattle. To get away from this nationalistic education and also from the Catholic Church, she had gone to the Sorbonne to study, had mastered French and Italian, and had married an Italian, a distinguished figure in the political and literary worlds. The younger woman, however, the daughter of an Irish patriot, who had served his term in prison and who had later been an official of the Irish republic, had been brought up on the ideals of Eire and had never reacted against them. For this young woman, Gaelic was a part of her creed, as was the right—and with this I did sympathize—of Ireland to stand out of the second war. She believed, I discovered, in a world entirely made up of many small nations, each speaking its own language—the more languages, apparently, the better. Uniformity was much to be dreaded—and, besides, if you had small countries, you would have, she thought, only small wars. Though she had lived several years in the United States, any other sort of political ideal was apparently unimaginable for her.

Now, was it possible, I asked myself, for *me*, to imagine the state of mind that had gone to produce *her* ideal? I realized that it was somewhat difficult for me to put myself in the place of a member of a small nation. We had suffered from the English in the early days, but we had beaten and expelled their forces, and, besides, we had ourselves been mainly English : we had not lost the national language. If one had suffered for centuries and had lost it, one might well behave like the Irish. There was, after all, the example at home of the South. The Southerners cherished still their old rage against the northern invaders, a stout and defiant loyalty to their antiquated limitations as well as to their traditional virtues which was not unlike that of the

Irish. Yet, a member myself of that power group which had subjected the South to its domination, I felt at moments the same sort of impatience with them as the British authorities felt with the Irishmen that shot their landlords. I could not help feeling annoyance that the South should keep on being silly. Yet to find oneself absorbed by a power unit can never be a pleasant experience, unless one be a born time-server or opportunist. In Europe, however, when the last war was over, both Germany and England had lost their positions, and France had already lost hers : there were no longer any big power magnets for the smaller units to cling to, and everything was flying to pieces. If one cultivated one's local language, one could try to make a cosy little world of one's own, in which everyone was everyone's friend, everyone was everyone's kinsman. They could keep one another alive and warm in the midst of the great desolation, which had looming on either side of it the threats of two terribly alien monsters : ourselves and the Soviet Union.

.   .   .

At the time when the United States was being flooded by refugees from Europe, we had to hear from them many complaints of the absence of culture in the United States—a condition which gave them pain. These complaints, to be sure, came often from persons who could themselves offer nothing but a parade of conventional opinions, who had been living in their various countries just as much unaware of contemporary creative forces—or just as supercilious about them—as they were of those in the United States, who hardly bothered to visit our galleries, our museums or our concert halls, and who sometimes did not know enough English to read American books. But some were distinguished people who simply could not rid themselves of the notion that Europe was the home of the arts and America a barbarian backwater. This attitude, for us, had its piquancy at a moment when so many of the best minds of Europe had fled to America for their souls or their lives, or had quietly, in earlier years, removed to the United States, where they found things more comfortable or freer. We had here in the States, during those years of the war, Einstein and Whitehead; Huxley, Auden and Isherwood; Thomas Mann, Vladimir

Nabokov, St.-John Perse and the Polish poet Julian Tuvim;
Schoenberg, Stravinsky, Bartók, Hindemith, Křenek and Milhaud;
Toscanini and Kusevitsky; Chelishchev, George Grosz and the
Surrealists; and how many lesser figures : the Molnars, the
Maughams, the Simenons; conductors, directors, actors. Some of
these became American citizens and are still living in the United
States. It was in Europe, though few would admit it, that the
barbaric age had begun, with the results foreseen by Gibbon. At
the end of Chapter XXXVIII of the *Decline and Fall: General
Observations on the Fall of The Roman Empire in the West,* he
discusses the possibility of new inroads of barbarism in Europe.
He is inclined to dismiss the danger of an invasion from the
direction of Russia, since—writing in the reign of Catherine the
Great—he believes that the improvements of "the science of war"
are likely to be "accompanied with a proportional improvement
in the arts of peace and civil policy. Yet this apparent security
should not tempt us to forget that new enemies and unknown
dangers, may *possibly* arise; and should the victorious barbarians
carry slavery and desolation as far as the Atlantic Ocean, ten
thousand vessels would transport beyond their pursuit the remains
of civilized society; and Europe would revive and flourish in the
American world, which is already filled with her colonies and
institutions."

.   .   .

A certain kind of European overrates the comparative importance, in the present age of the world, of a good deal of his cultural
tradition, and often of his own real interest in it. For myself, as an
American, I have not the least doubt that I have derived a good
deal more benefit of the civilizing as well as of the inspirational
kind from the admirable American bathroom than I have from
the cathedrals of Europe. I do not, of course, deny the impressive-
ness or the many varied beauties of these monuments, nor their
usefulness to the people in their time; I have enjoyed their delightful coolness and their shade from the glare of the sun on broiling
days in France and Italy—though in cold weather they are
likely to be unbearable. But I have had a good many more
uplifting thoughts, creative and expansive visions—while soaking in

comfortable baths or drying myself after bracing showers—in well-equipped American bathrooms than I have ever had in any cathedral. Here the body purges itself, and along with the body, the spirit. Here the mind becomes free to ruminate, to plan ambitious projects. The cathedrals, with their distant domes, their long aisles and their high groinings, do add stature to human strivings; their chapels do give privacy for prayer. But the bathroom, too, shelters the spirit, it tranquillizes, and reassures, in surroundings of a celestial whiteness, where the pipes and the faucets gleam and the mirror makes another liquid surface, which will render you, shaved, rubbed and brushed, a nobler and more winning appearance. Here, too, you may sing, recite, refresh yourself with brief readings, just as you do in church; and the fact that you do it without a priest and not as a member of a congregation is, from my point of view, an advantage. It encourages self-dependence and prepares one to face the world, fortified, firm on one's feet, serene and with a mind like a diamond.

.   .   .

Yet I find that today, at sixty, I sometimes feel a certain yearning for London, Paris and Rome. Though I had seen something of Europe in my youth, I did not go there at all in the fourteen years between 1921 and 1935, and in '35 I only passed through it on my way to and from Russia. It was not till 1945 that I spent any time again in the European countries, and then, at the end of the second war, they were battered and grisly, demoralized. Coming back through Paris, however, on my trip of 1954, I found that I enormously enjoyed the moderately priced champagne and the crisp and salty *pommes de terre frites* in the Café Voltaire on the Quai Voltaire (though the Germans, it was sad to see, had destroyed the Voltaire statue), and was reminded of my dinners, during the first of the wars, at hotels in the snowy Vosges. We would walk to some dark old château on the brink of the Black Forest and buy up the small stock of champagne that would always be on hand in the village inn, or we would sit getting warm in the old-fashioned kitchen of the Hôtel de France in Vittel, watching the soup being heated in a great copper pot. After my years of concentration—from the beginning of the

twenties—on the United States and Soviet Russia, I indulged, on
this last trip, the illusion of visiting again the Paris and London
of my youth. I took my six-year-old daughter to the Tower of
London and the Christmas pantomime and—failing the old
Maskelyne Temple of Magic—to a performance by the current
Maskelyne which seemed to me quite first rate, well up to the
family tradition. I went the rounds of the bookshops in the Charing
Cross Road—near which Harold Monro had had his Poetry Book-
shop, where I once heard Rupert Brooke read—and of those of the
Avenue de l'Opéra, where, in 1919, I had found it thrilling to see
the then so cheap many-volumed sets with pasteboard placards
announcing the prices. I took lunch in the Rue de Rivoli at one
of those restaurants with plush-covered seats, the same one, I
thought, that a cousin and I—fascinated by the *pommes de terre
soufflées* : we couldn't see how it was done—had, in the summer
of 1908, visited again and again. I took my daughter to the Cirque
Médrano; but where were the London Music Halls? Where were
the Paris Guitrys? Sacha Guitry, playing Louis XIV, we found in
a dreadful film—a glorification of French history called *Si
Versailles M'Était Conté* : very funny but not meant to be, a
pageant which for comprehensiveness made *Savonarola Brown*
look perfunctory. Bossuet and Fénelon preach (the latter, played
by Jean Barrault, turns out to be an accomplished pantomimist).
Fersen is seen in the company of Marie Antoinette; Molière kisses
Armande Béjard. A series of couples at the King's masked ball all
turn out to be famous people : one is Marivaux, who unmasks and
exchanges with his partner some marivaudage; another is
Fragonard—"Oh," exclaims Pompadour, his partner, when she
finds out who he is, "you must paint me!" Immediately, you see
him painting her. Voltaire happens to be there, and when the
King drops in on them, too, the great sceptic makes some sceptical
remarks about the economic situation of France. Lavoisier, André
Chénier and Robespierre all—by a curious coincidence, full of
dramatic irony—call at the Palace the same afternoon, and discuss
with Louis XVI and Marie Antoinette the abolition of capital
punishment : they are agreed that they would hate to be executed.
D'Artagnan pleases Louis XIV by a characteristic gesture of
bravery; Orson Welles appears as Franklin and makes him seem

rather sinister; Edith Piaf sings *Ça Ira*; Louis XIV, making an exit in a wheeled chair, snatches, in passing, a bit of paper from a man who is standing by: *"Monsieur de Saint-Simon,"* he says, *"vous avez l'habitude déplorable de rapporter inexactement les paroles et les personages!"* Sacha Guitry plays the old Louis XIV in a cold and monotonous manner that suggests that he is really playing Lucien, his father, playing Louis XIV, with nuances learned from Louis Jouvet. The Montespan is Claudette Colbert, who invests her with a thoroughgoing vulgarity, intended, without a doubt, to make the picture attractive to the United States.—Well, here was our poor dear old Europe self-consciously strutting her stuff. Yet I was glad to see Guitry again, and I really didn't care in the least whether or not he had been friendly with the Germans.

V

Russia

THE FINE PHOTOGRAPHS by Cartier-Bresson of the ordinary people in Soviet Russia I found, in their implications— from the point of view of progress—extremely depressing. The men and women on the streets of Moscow seemed not to have changed in the least since I had been there twenty years before. They looked just as amorphous, stunted, badly cared-for and badly dressed. They appeared just as much at sea, just as lacking in self-assurance, just as little as if they had any grip on the society in which they lived, any share in the direction of their lives. A Russian woman who had been in Moscow when I was there in 1935 but who married an American and came to America has told me that these photographs have made upon her exactly the same impression : she had felt, she said, a sad discouragement.

The main thing to understand in accounting for Soviet Russia is the fact that it is now composed almost exclusively of the least enlightened elements of old Russia : that vast peasant population, whom Lenin idealized and in whom he desired to awake the consciousness of playing an "historic rôle," but who were long to remain, if no longer illiterate, very limited in their access to the world of print, and primitive in their habits, unorganized in their own communities and with no kind of political experience to enable them to govern themselves. The Westernizing nobility of Russia were driven out at the time of the Revolution; the revolutionary "intelligentsia" were speedily destroyed by Stalin, and—in fear for his own position—he succeeded as long as he lived, through the turnover effected by his purges, in preventing the perpetuation of an hereditary upper class with special privileges and better education. Stalin himself—an unusual man, so conspicuously gifted as a tyrant that he commanded for his miserable country a certain blood-chilling respect—has now passed from the Soviet scene, and we are confronted, and shall no doubt be confronted long, with such leaders, mere routine top officials, as these hounded potato-faced crowds—individually so capable of charm, so heroically resistant to invasion, yet so ignorant of the modern world—have been able, from their own ranks, to breed and train. The drive and high purpose of Lenin, the intellectual brilliance of Trotsky, the incredible cynicism and cruelty of Stalin, have invested the leadership of the Soviet Union with a prestige which it is unlikely to sustain. It seems evident that the only departments in which, at the present time, it is possible to excel in Russia are those of the mechanical arts, with their henchmen of chemistry and physics.

. . .

We are used to mediocrity in the United States. I have described above our low-calibre presidents—they, too, are more or less astute party hacks. And the Soviet Union and the United States do have certain things in common which they do not have in common with Europe : the big country, the pioneering, the fraternal informal manners, the federation of varied peoples, the tendency to settle standards on the level of the "common man." What is, of course, on the part of the Russians, fundamentally different from us is their complete lack of training in democratic institutions, their heritage of autocratic rule. One of the first things in Soviet Russia that strikes a modern American—because it annoys him and holds him up—is the usual incapacity of the average person to make any sort of decision for himself. The Russian hates responsibility, always wants to pass problems along to somebody higher up, who will pass them on to someone higher. For such people, at their present stage, a dictatorship is surely inevitable : it did not take Marx to supply it. The visiting American realizes that democracy in the United States depends on a sharing of responsibility of a kind that the Russians cannot even imagine, which begins with such to us simple matters—made so difficult in

Soviet Russia—as cashing a cheque at a bank or selling a railway ticket. And where the processes do not work smoothly, where the routine co-ordination fails, their procedure is different from ours. You are walked on in the Soviet Union or you walk over other people. If you get on the wrong side of authority, you are executed or exiled, crushed; whereas here in the United States we have showdowns, slugging it out, battles between pickets and police, filibusterings of Bills in Congress, earnest arguments before the Supreme Court. Instead of settling conflicts of interest by irrevocable dismissals and sweeping proscriptions, we give vent to our violence as we go along, relieve our crises of friction in innumerable limited contests.

.   .   .

This mixture of what is familiar with what is unfamiliar to Americans is officially presented to the rest of the world by the spokesmen for the Soviet Union in the unfamiliar language of Marxism, which is here deprived of plausibility by being used—not, as Marx intended, as an instrument of social analysis—but as a kind of mumbo-jumbo to justify whatever current policy the government happens to find expedient. The average American, thus, does not know how to take the Russians. He is so far deceived by the Russian claim to be practising Marxist socialism that the dominating element in his attitude is likely to be the traditional fear, characteristic of the American businessman, of government ownership or interference. This leads him completely to identify modern socialism and the Soviet dictatorship, with its slave labour and secret police, its lack of due process of law, its government edicts and one-candidate balloting. He blames upon socialism all these features of Russian life which have always existed in Russia and which the democratic ideals of Lenin—who expected the State to "wither away"—were unable to get rid of in a generation. The ordinary citizen of the United States has usually failed to recognize how much—for better or worse—the States and the Soviet Union have been influencing one another. When I visited the Soviet Union in 1935, I found an admiration for the United States—our industry and the comforts it produced—which, rather to my surprise, seemed far to surpass the hostility which these nurselings of Lenin were supposed to feel towards American capitalism. I remember a Soviet writer inquiring—as if thrilled by the idea of this—whether the novelist John Dos Passos did not possess two cars. And we, on our side, have aped the Russians. The policies of the New Deal—with its projects for government-owned utilities, its restrictions on the output of agriculture and its efforts at long-range planning—would, I believe, not have taken the direction they did if it had not been for the example of the Soviet Five-Year Plans. We have also been copying the Russians in less constructive ways. Our recent security purges and political heresy-hunts must have been partly inspired by the Russian trials. We have suffered, as I have said above, from periodical frights of this kind; but this last has been characterized by features that have not appeared before, or not to the same degree: the imputation of guilt by association, the effort to incriminate people through the supposed Leftist leanings of their relatives and friends; and the branding as traitorous activity not merely of "subversive" ideas but of any unconventional opinion on politics, morals or even æsthetics. It is typical of what has been going on that one of the most distinguished of our immigrant writers should, in taking out citizen's papers, have not only been catechized on his soundness in the matter of "premature anti-fascism"—which meant objecting to Hitler before we were actually at war with him, an attitude regarded as sinister, a probable indication of a sympathy with Communism—but asked, with a suggestion of menace, whether he thought it was possible "to make the world a better place to live in." In our nationalist propaganda, we have lately been vying with the Russians in an ostrich-like and naïve absurdity. There is the affair of the photograph of the "Little Red Schoolhouse, 1750." This appeared as an illustration in a book called *Profile of America* which it was proposed to include in a programme of "information for propaganda overseas"; but this selection was blocked by a Senate committee, on the ground, as the author was told, that the Russians might be led to suppose that this modest old-fashioned building "represented" the American "school system." The author of the *Profile*, Miss Emily Ravie, was also admonished against "the photograph of a dust storm and arid land." "Are we not," she asks, "to have dust in America? Two pages back I have shown

T.V.A., an engineering feat that other countries might well admire and copy to combat the problems of flood and drought every country must be enduring." The senators, it seems, approved of a photograph of a modern school, more impressively constructed of concrete. Yet the opposite principle—which plays up the more primitive as against the more advanced institution—appears to have operated in another case, in which our U.S. officialdom does not seem to have fallen far short of the practice of imposture by concealment that has long been standard procedure in the Soviet Union in its guided tours for foreign observers. When a delegation of Russian farm experts were visiting us in the summer of 1955 and travelling through the Middle West under the tutelage of the Department of Agriculture, they were, I am told, taken only to see small or moderate-sized farms—none larger than a hundred and sixty acres—in order that they might not learn that we, also, did large-scale farming of the kind that is cultivated in Communist Russia. It was only by chance, in Iowa, that the Russians got wind of the large-scale operations of Mr. Roswell Garst, and only with the greatest difficulty that they obtained permission to see them. What they found was a revelation. This farm included twenty-five hundred acres, and it was producing the best type of the new hybrid corn, sometimes at the staggering rate of a hundred bushels an acre. The Garsts had also developed a new method of feeding cattle on ground-up corn-cobs and corn stalks mixed with urea and molasses, and a new use of nitrogen fertilizer. Mr. Garst, as a result of the visit, was invited to inspect Russian farms, and this he has been permitted to do. But the Russians want to buy from him his hybrid corn, and there is now, in certain quarters here, much alarm lest their use of this, by raising their standard of living, may strengthen their hand against us. The Garst farm has been treated, in fact, as if it were virtually a laboratory for making the hydrogen bomb.

•   •   •

We have been much too much afraid of the Russians, and have allowed ourselves frequently to be bluffed by them. But it is not only their communism that has made us so skittish : it is our apprehension of something more alien, something deeply antipathetic to ourselves. Mr. Stewart Alsop, for example, recently returning from the Soviet Union, has declared that he felt in Russia the presence of elements he could not understand and never would understand, and that some of our official representatives said they shared with him this feeling of bafflement. I think I know what he means, but it is not so much that Russia is inexplicable as that even an intelligent American finds it difficult to believe that a people existing in the twentieth century can get through their lives as the Russians do or that the affairs of so important a country can be carried on in the Russian way. It is something of what people mean by, and what the Russians themselves used to talk about as, the oriental side of Russia; it is what is meant, also, when people say that Russia is Byzantine. It is probably much easier for the foreigner to get the hang of the countries that are truly and frankly oriental, to take them on their own terms. The alien elements of the Soviet Union affect him as disquieting, uncanny, because they turn up in fusion with pretences at Western discipline, Western logic and organization. This is, of course, an old enough story; but let me give a specific example of a reaction to this aspect of Russia by an observer, more experienced than Alsop, of seventy-five years ago. The Vicomte Melchior de Vogüé was an old-fashioned French Royalist diplomat, able, high-minded and somewhat adventurous, who served in the French embassy in St. Petersburg from 1876 to 1883. He married a Russian wife, learned Russian extremely well and published *Le Roman Russe*—probably the best book on Russian literature that has ever been written by a foreigner. Vogüé was in residence in Petersburg at the time of the assassination of Alexander II in 1881, and he set down in his diary a vivid account of the events that followed this. First, the calm on the part of the people that succeeded this hideous deed of violence—the Tsar had been bombed in his carriage and both his legs blown off without his being immediately killed : "The people in the streets have their usual air, tranquil and indolent. No curiosity, no emotion in their faces. A strange people!" But "the panic," he writes on March 18th, "is everywhere increasing in the Imperial Family and in society." When, the next day, the body of the Emperor is transported to the Fortress of Peter and Paul, "in that long parade," he notes, "from 11 o'clock in the morning to 3, not a detail really great or really touching; a bad operatic ensemble, with an archaism that drives away even the possibility of meditation or grief. These heralds, these men-at-arms with gilded breast-plates, these coats of arms, these crowns and orders carried by eighth-grade functionaries, all this is too remote from our modern customs to be associated with a real and present grief. . . . The dead man is received with the magnificent Orthodox chant. Fascinating face of an old archimandrite, the head of an ascetic stepped down from one of the ikons of Athos, with a macabre flame of life in his lean body : how he makes me understand the holy idiots of the Middle Ages ! On the dais of cloth of gold they lay this poor lacerated corpse, disguised and dissimulated in wrappings of cloth and tulle. The jaw has fallen loose on the way. All about this amputated torso, the orders, the crowns, the insignia worn by the high officers : Chuvalov, the unfortunate negotiator of Berlin, holds the sword of Russia. After the ceremony everybody goes to kiss the coffin; some of the women weep, including my wife; but there is nothing that is really touching, too many goings and comings, too much chatter and distraction in the church." Three days later : "The panic continues, mass arrests. . . . The unfortunate Emperor is literally prisoner in his palace. He is not even allowed to go out in the evening to pray at his father's tomb. Squads of Cossacks guard him from view. The criminals, turning the tables, have put the Sovereign in prison." Two days later : "The scientists are applying the latest advances in chemistry, the pyroxylines and other things, to the destruction of the reigning power : this power tries to make them talk, once they are caught, by means of the latest advances in magnetism and electricity. . . . They are men of the Middle Ages, with medieval passions—which are mental ailments—that make use of these marvellous inventions. They have cut off, embalmed and preserved, for future confrontations, the head of the unknown who died in the hospital [one of the conspirators, who had killed himself]. All this is more monstrous than nature. What dramas could be made of it ! How it beats the sixteenth century and the Borgias !" "March 27th. Funeral of the Emperor. Cursed weather, violent north wind. All the princes of the earth, heirs apparent of Germany, England and Denmark, the Archduke Charles-Louis, a horde of little Germans. Magnificent liturgical pomp. Tragic thoughts in that church : the three layers : the courtiers above, given up to their intrigues and their greeds; the corpses buried in the earth; the condemned below the ground, in the casemates, cursing the others—that is the real crime, this hate which is fermenting beneath our feet. A horrible world, deformed, while the priests are singing, 'Glory to God!' Talked with Polovtsov, with Lieven; disorder, unrest and vague mental disquiet in the provinces." "March 31st. Departure of the burdensome guests. Petersburg empties itself of its princes and their foreign uniforms. Life resumes, but is streaked with the terrors and the efforts in the void of this moment." "April 8th. We are received in audience at the Anichkov Palace, at one o'clock, to serve as a screen for the mysterious departure to Gachina. The Emperor appears in Cossack dress, tall, fat, heavy, shy, awkward in person and speech. He says a few hasty words to the chiefs of mission; the Empress retrieves a little this impression of embarrassment. In her retiring room, behind the door, the little heads of the tragic children watch curiously all these dubious foreigners. Framed in the entrance door, one can see—parading and laughing—the evil genius of the future reign, General Ignatiev, yesterday appointed, in Lieven's place, Minister of the Domains." "April 10th. Only this morning, at half past six, after seventeen hours of sittings, the High Court of the Senate has finally handed down the verdict, condemning the six accused to the gallows. The gas has been put out; the dawn gave a yellow tinge to all of our livid faces, fatigued from sitting up all night. A sinister picture. The condemned were superb. They kissed one another, smiling. . . . The bench of the prosecution and the bench of the defence : there, a few peasants, with an absolute idea, an absolute energy; here the formidable power, but without idea or energy." "April 15th. Execution of the five condemned. . . . A few arrests in the crowd, in general very quiet. A day that weighed upon one, a heavy and painful feeling over everybody and everything.—April 16th. Everyone in the city is blundering about. Most unlikely stories of outrages, captures, new measures. They are all waiting for something that will reassure them : a man, an idea, an act of the Power, and the Power remains silent, enigmatic, invisible in its burrow of Gachina. Precious hours lost—the process of disorganization is, it seems to me, taking place in full view."

As a Frenchman—though himself a Royalist—Vogüé is appalled by Imperial Russia : its emptiness, inaction and terror, the ineptitude, the bad taste of this Byzantine court, which is trying to adapt its procedure to the ideals of its Western education. In France, they would carry on; here everything comes to a standstill. There is no firm machinery of government to keep operating through accidents and breakdowns. Instead, there are intrigues, conspiracies, scandals of passion, proscriptions, and, on a gigantic scale, bribes and embezzlements—the foreigner from the West, like Alsop, finds he cannot even guess at the kind of thing that is going on. It was the same in the imperial household in the days of Rasputin's black magic and of the butchering of him by Yusupov. It was the same in the Kremlin of Stalin. In one of Vogüé's later writings, he touches on another phenomenon which has behind it the same mentality that so shocked him at the Russian court. He is trying—in an article in *La Revue des Deux Mondes* of 1902—to write for the French about Chekhov. He had been horrified, again, to realize that it was possible for a Russian dramatist to say, in effect, to his audience : " 'Come : I propose to amuse you by showing you everything that is dreariest, everything that is most boring, in your country, in the routine of your daily life; you all of you aspire, as my heroes do, to get out of this dismal swamp : I am going to plunge you for several hours back into this slough along with them; and I shall prove to you that it is quite impossible for you ever to pull yourselves out of it.' This showman of self-annihilation has actually made good his claim : to the mirror that Chekhov holds up Russia comes to see how much she is bored; she applauds the reflection of a reality which she declares to be thoroughly stultifying. I simply state without understanding." When young Treplev in *The Seagull* shoots himself, the Frenchman's sense of logic is offended : "Nothing has prepared us for so tragic an end; it is difficult for us to fathom the disjointed feelings of these characters." And Chekhov himself, he says, "is not aroused, does not protest."

Vogüé has reached the conclusion that the state of mind of the Russians has a good deal in common with Buddhism : an indifference to practical results, a detachment from material conditions; yet finds difficulty in reconciling this with their progress as "a vigorous young nation, which is becoming every day more avid to acquire our civilization and more skilful in making use of it . . . the progress she is making in the world is directed with a vigilance and a method which give proof of a practical sense as well as of her force of expansion. Here are signs of vitality which are hardly consistent with the contemplation of the navel; the seal of the Buddhist renunciation is scarcely to be discerned on the visage of the Russia that works and conquers." This is the paradox of Russia still. We sympathize—as our engineers did when they were employed by the Soviets in the twenties—with the eagerness of the Russians to build and to win. We are put off by the Buddhist and the Byzantine side; and, as I say, it was this, I imagine, that so puzzled Mr. Alsop when he was trying to get some idea of what was going on in Moscow. It ought to be added that the Soviet Buddhist and the Soviet Byzantine is also a master of chess. In the midst of his corruption and inertia, he enjoys working out clever moves and witnessing his opponent's discomfiture.

Though I personally like Russians extremely—sharing with them a certain indifference to the mechanical efficiency of the West as well as their intellectual appetite—and though I greatly admire their art, there are moments, nevertheless—after a prolonged immersion, say, in Mussorgsky's music or in one of the nineteenth century novelists—when I feel, like M. de Vogüé, a kind of disgust and revulsion. *Boris Godunov,* one of the greatest of operas, per-haps the greatest opera of its century—with its idiot, its sinister bells, its story of the blood-stained Tsar, demoralized by the threat of a claimant who is himself an audacious impostor, the barbaric palace : a prison of guilt, the horror that hangs over its nursery—in the end, it makes us want to refresh ourselves with the bell-clear melodies of Mozart or even with Wagner's heroics. And the swinish back-country of Gogol, full of overeaten landowners and overgrown orchards, wretched slaves and maniacal masters; the old nests of gentlefolks of Turgenev, with their messiness of family relations and their herds of ill-treated serfs—one may be glad to get away to Jane Austen. Lenin, of course, declared war on all this, and the Communists have made efforts to clear it away. But they are Rus-sians, and must work in the Russian tongue, with the habits and the mentality that have made it. Their language, so brilliantly expressive, so rich in vocabulary and idiom, so varied in verbal nuances, so wonderful for poetry and drama, is less suited to practical uses. In the hands of its great writers, it never becomes formal or dry: it lives wherever you touch it. Yet it is clumsy for the clear presentation of summarized data or logical analysis, for arguments, transactions, reports. How to construct a precision instrument out of the rank and tangled materials of one of those old Russian gardens—full of creepers and ferns and moss, where nothing has been pruned or trimmed, where the paths have not been smoothed with gravel, where the flower beds do not make patterns—which merge with a forest of birch-trees? And add to this unkempt, untended, this grammatically anarchical Russian tongue the jargon of German Marxism: no simile can cope with the situation! You have a medium that acts by itself as a block to communication, that itself makes an iron curtain.

●   ●   ●

Even well-informed reporters, then, who are sent to the Soviet Union are likely to come back bewildered. It has only been lately that the United States has been able to provide trained diplomats —George F. Kennan and Charles E. Bohlen—who know Russian and Russia well, who are equipped to get the hang of what is happening there. It may be noted that an early reaction to this on the part of the Soviet rulers has been to declare Mr. Kennan *persona non grata* in Moscow.

A Later Bulletin

Since the notes above were written, the Soviet line has been somewhat changed. The reputation of Stalin has been dethroned, and his blunders as a statesman have been denounced as well as his atrocities as a tyrant. The power of the secret police to judge and execute *in camera* has been abolished, and judicial procedure restored. The frame-ups of Stalin are acknowledged, and some at least of the political prisoners are being set free and exonerated. The Soviet leaders are travelling abroad and trying to make conciliatory gestures, and foreigners are being invited to visit the Soviet Union.

There has always been a tendency in Russia to alternate periods of self-containment and refusal to traffic with the West with periods of an eagerness to learn from the more advanced civilizations and a relative freedom of intercourse with them. The first kind of policy is likely to imply a phase of reaction at home, and the latter a phase of reform. The Westernizing of Peter and Catherine the Great and the intermediate monarch was continued by the cosmopolitanism of Alexander I, which encouraged the cosmopolitanism of a Pushkin. But the reign of Nicholas I began with the hanging of the Decembrist leaders who had asked for a constitution, and went on to the organization of a new and more formidable secret police and the suppression or expulsion of the Westernizing liberals. The succession of Alexander II brought a swing in the other direction : the emancipation of the serfs, the setting up of courts of law whose proceedings took place in public—as has just been done again, after the relapse of the Stalin régime into the habits of pre-1855—and of trial by jury for criminal cases, the institution of a system of local self-government, the encouragement of foreign capital and the admission of the Jews to the liberal professions. But the murder of Alexander II provoked another reign of terror on the part of Alexander III, who did away with the independence of the law-courts and the universities, extinguished the minority languages, demoted and massacred the Jews, and set on the secret police to round up the liberals and ship them to Siberia. Nicholas II, in his feebler way, more or less carried on this policy; then the Bolshevik Revolution of 1917 created a new situation, in the development of which, however, the old oscillations continued. When Kirov, the president of the Leningrad Soviet, began to emerge in the early thirties as a relatively liberal leader who showed signs of promoting a transition—after the bitterness and self-discipline of the Revolution—into a period of greater comfort, more democratic methods and a more international culture, he was—apparently with Stalin's connivance—very quickly assassinated, and revolutionary Russia fell back into the pre-Petrine darkness of Ivan the Terrible, who was now made a national hero. Recently, since Stalin's death, a movement in the other direction has been getting under way. We, too, as I have noted above, have experienced, in our milder terms, periodical alternations between xenophobe and xenophile phases. We have lately been making difficulties about passports—not merely keeping foreigners out but even forbidding our own citizens to travel in foreign countries— very much in the Russian fashion.

VI

The Jews

I HAVE HAD, in the course of my reading, three somewhat similar experiences. It happened that I had never read Voltaire till after I already knew well the work of a number of writers— Stendhal, Flaubert, Anatole France—who owed a good deal to his spirit and tone. These are all, in their various fashions, deliberately artistic writers in a way that Voltaire was not. They are predominantly novelists and aphorists, whereas Voltaire was a fast-producing journalist, with a style based on conversation. In Voltaire, the bright mocking attack is something so completely natural that ironic effects do not need to be built up; the witticisms are never planted: they are spontaneous and over in a flash, like the quick striking of a match, almost before the reader knows it. One realized that here was the essence—in its free original form—of an element one had only encountered as the leaven in substantial loaves.

When, later on, I came to read Pushkin, I recognized that here was the artistic model as well as the humane spirit that had dominated Russian literature. The foreigner who does not know this model is likely to remain unaware of certain of the admirable qualities that make the Russian writers he does know effective. It has been usual for Western readers to assume in the case of Turgenev that he must owe his perfect balance and his nice sense of form, his restraint and his ironic portraiture, to imitation of Western models. But all this is to be found in Pushkin, and nothing could be more misleading than the belief, so prevalent abroad, that it is typical of Russian literature to be formless, prolix and hysterical. The reader of translations from the Russian can know nothing of Russian poetry, which has never lost Pushkin's mould : a classical regularity and a concise epigrammatic turn that make the quatrains of A. E. Housman peculiarly congenial to Russians. In fiction, the Western critic—who has concluded from Constance Garnett's translations that Russian novelists all write very much alike—pushes Turgenev aside as an exception; takes Gogol as a gross *farçeur*, a kind of prose Russian Rowlandson; regards Tolstoy as the lavish compiler of an uneven and fatiguing epic and Dostoevsky as an inspired madman. Henry James's strictures on the Russians are typical of the Western attitude : Tolstoy and Dostoevsky are "fluid puddings, though not tasteless . . . thanks to the strong rank quality of their genius and their experience . . . we see how great a vice is their lack of composition, their defiance of economy and architecture"; "I have been reading over Tolstoy's interminable *War and Peace*. . . . He doesn't *do* to read over, and that exactly is the answer to those who idiotically proclaim the impunity of such formless shape, such flopping looseness and such a denial of composition, selection and style." Yet *War and Peace,* which was several times rewritten and from which Tolstoy eliminated about a third of the original material, is a masterpiece of economy and organization. Like the prose and verse tales of Pushkin and his miniature dramas in verse, each one of Tolstoy's little episodes exactly makes its picture, its point, and none of them is allowed to go on too long. In the balance of personalities that provides the system of stresses and strains on which the novel rests, Tolstoy also follows the Pushkinian tradition—established in *Evgeni Onegin*—which gives its structure to Turgenev's work. The devotion and sobriety of Princess Marie set off the electric vitality and the reckless self-abandonment of Natasha; the three men—Pierre, Prince André and Nikolai Rostov—maintain a steady equilibrium between three fundamental types : the idealist inept at life, the serious and responsible aristocrat and the non-intellectual natural man. There is, also, in Tolstoy as in Pushkin, a detached and ironical point of view that is closer to the comic than the tragic, and which even the self-righteous moralizing that commences in *Anna Karenina* can never entirely destroy. Dostoevsky *is* really diffuse, a creator through whom his creation is rushing to get itself down; but his work is not in the least, as Hugh Walpole, in reply to the complaints above, called it in a letter to Henry James, a "mad jumble that flings things down in a heap." You have also in Dostoevsky the balance of personalities : Myshkin and Rogozhin in *The Idiot,* the three brothers Karamazov, representing a different trinity from Tolstoy's; and you have also a dramatization which seems to me much more objective, rather closer to the ideal of comedy than to the traditional pattern of tragedy—in spite of the horrors involved—than even many Russians grant. I felt this in Dostoevsky before I had ever read Pushkin; but the reading of Pushkin confirmed it and enabled me to appreciate, in general, the classicism of Russian literature : the clear observation, the matching of opponents, the coolness of resolution.

A similar revelation comes out of the Hebrew Bible. The Hebrew religious conceptions, the imagery of the Hebrew scriptures have been an element of literature in English from the King James translation on. This is, of course, especially strong in Milton, who knew Hebrew at first hand; but the pregnant phrases of the Bible, its apocalyptic visions, are a part of the texture of our language. The culture of no other Western people seems so deeply to have been influenced by these : something in the English character, something mystical, tough and fierce, has a special affinity to Hebrew. Yet the strong Hebrew strain in English is to some extent at variance with the influence of the Greek and Roman tradition. In proportion as one inclines towards this latter, one is likely to resent the other. In my own case, I followed, in my youth, the line of reaction then common against old-fashioned Bible-worship, the recoil from the rigours of Calvinism. Yet my grandfather on my father's side was a Presbyterian minister, though a very moderate one, and when my parents went to church on Sunday, they would leave me with my formidable grandmother, who undertook my instruction in the Scriptures. These bleak and severe Sunday mornings, though they left me with a respect for the Bible, had the effect of antagonizing me against it, and this attitude was tacitly encouraged by the moral sabotage of my mother, whose family, once rigorous New Englanders, had scrapped the old-time religion and still retained a certain animus towards it. At college, I was enchanted by classical Greek, and, though I made a point of reading through the Gospels, I told myself how immeasurably much I preferred Socrates to Jesus. Later on, I elected the second half of a course in Old Testament literature. I already admired Ecclesiastes, and—though finding Ezekiel tedious—I tried to do justice to the Prophets. It was not till much later, in my fifties, that I acquired a little Hebrew, and, for a third time, I had the experience of finding myself in contact with something in its pure and original form that I had previously only known in compounds or adaptations. The strangeness of this element in English became a good deal more comprehensible when one was able to take account, not only of the structural differences between the Semitic languages and the Teutonic and Latin ones, but also of the difference from ours of the oriental way of apprehending the world that these structural divergences reflected. I have written about this elsewhere at length, so I merely want here to note that an acquaintance with the Hebrew Bible is at once to make the Biblical narratives sound a good deal more simple and natural—the archaic Jacobean English still today partly screens them from us—and to compel one to pay attention to certain fundamental discrepancies between the Hebrew way of thinking and ours. The language of Jehovah and his worshippers, which seems in English grandiose and mysterious, may not, even in Gesenius' dictionary, become to us readily intelligible and render itself in familiar terms; but here at least we can meet at first hand this vocabulary and these locutions, try to form some idea of their meaning to the men who first coined and employed them to deal with their objective and subjective worlds—or rather, with the moral continuum that embraced the phenomena of both. It is useful to approach the Bible with a scholarly dictionary and commentary—for otherwise it is bound, more or less, to remain an esoteric text, a repository of tales for children, a dream book, a compendium of incantations. The Jews—who have lost touch with the original text—have been interpreting it for a couple of thousand years in ever more far-fetched and fantastic ways. The Christians have been equally fantastic—beginning with the extravagances of Justin Martyr—in reading back into it the coming of Christ; and the old lady who was infinitely grateful for that blessed word *Mesopotamia* was only an extreme case of the Christian dependence on Scripture for this sort of consolation. Some of the oddest features of the Bible, as we get it through our Jacobean version, are simply due to mistranslations. So Joseph's coat of many colours was in reality a coat with long sleeves; so Moses had sprouting from his head, not horns, but rays of light. Yet the horns of Moses and the many-coloured coat are as hard to get out of one's head, unless one sees what they are in the original, as the images in nursery rhymes. Many mysteries, of course, remain. Some are puzzles of vocabulary or grammar : there are, in the text of the Bible, something like five hundred words that do not occur anywhere else, and the copyists have made mistakes. But it is difficult, also, to adjust oneself to certain fundamental features of the Hebrew way of looking at things, and, though there is constant speculation on these matters, they are now so remote from our habits of thought that some scholars believe we must give them up. In any case, we find here—with the language they have minted —the religio-legal codes and the lofty prophetic poetry, the wisdom derived from experience and the permanently significant legends, the influence of which, refracted by the organisms of other mentalities, have reached distant countries and distant times. Here it is, that old tongue, with its clang and its flavour, sometimes rank, sometimes sweet, sometimes bitter; here it is in its concise solid stamp. Other cultures have felt its impact, and none—in the West at least—seems quite to accommodate it. Yet we find we have been living with it all our lives.

. . .

Thus the Gentile of American Puritan stock who puts himself in contact with the Hebrew culture finds something at once so alien that he has to make a special effort in order to adjust himself to it, and something that is perfectly familiar. The Puritanism of New England was a kind of new Judaism, a Judaism transposed into Anglo-Saxon terms. These Protestants, in returning to the text of the Bible, had concentrated on the Old Testament, and some had tried to take it as literally as any Orthodox Jew. The Judaic observances in New England were reduced to honouring the Sabbath on Sunday, but the attendance at the house of worship and the cessation from work on this day approached in their rigour the Jewish practice; and in England "certain extremists," says Mr.

Cecil Roth, in his *History of the Jews in England*, had "regarded the 'old' dispensation as binding, and even reverted to its practices of circumcision and the observance of the seventh-day Sabbath. In 1600, the Bishop of Exeter complained of the prevalence of 'Jewism' in his diocese, and such views were comparatively common in London and the Eastern counties. Numerous persons were prosecuted here for holding what were termed 'Judaistic' opinions, based on the literal interpretations of the Old Testament. As late as 1612, two so-called Aryans died at the stake (the last persons to suffer capital punishment in England purely for their religion) for teaching views regarding the nature of God which approximated to those of Judaism. The followers of the Puritan extremist, John Traske, went so far on the path of literalism that they were imprisoned in 1618–20 on a charge of Judaizing. In this case, the accusation was so far from being exaggerated that a number of them settled in Amsterdam and formally joined the synagogue."

When the Puritans came to America, they identified George III with Pharaoh and themselves with the Israelites in search of the Promised Land. They called their new country Canaan and talked continually of the Covenant they had made with God. Winthrop and Bradford were Moses and Joshua; Anne Hutchinson was pilloried as Jezebel. "The Christian church so-called," said a preacher in New Marlborough, Massachusetts, "is only a continuation and extension of the Jewish church." "If we keep this covenant," said Winthrop, "we shall find then the God of Israel is among us." The Hebrew language, later on in New England, was to be taught as a major subject, not merely in the colleges but even in the schools.

All this, of course, is well enough known. There is an interesting chapter on the subject—to which I am indebted for the facts above —in a volume by various hands called *The Hebrew Impact on Western Civilization—Hebraic Foundations of American Democracy* by Abraham I. Katsh. Yet we tend to forget how close our original relationship was to the Old Testament Jewish tradition. Our conception itself of America as a country with a mission in the world comes down to us from our Mosaic ancestors. We are told by Harriet Beecher Stowe that she had always felt in her childhood, after reading Cotton Mather's *Magnalia*, that "the very ground I stood on [in New England] was consecrated by some special dealing of God's providence"; and, even in our own time, Santayana, in *The Last Puritan,* has made one of his New England characters say : "We were always a circumcised people, consecrated to great expectations." The Gentile American however, is no longer aware of this in his attitude towards Judaism, and the American Jew does not recognize in what is left of the Puritan tradition a Gentile imitation of Judaism. I have recently been collecting examples of the persistence through the nineteenth century of the New Englander's deep-rooted conviction that the Jews are a special people selected for a unique rôle by God, and that New England somehow shares this destiny.

Perhaps the most curious of these is the rabbinical metamorphosis of the Hebrew scholar Calvin Ellis Stowe, the husband of Harriet Beecher. That Harriet was herself very close to the Pilgrims' self-identification with Israel is indicated not merely by the passage above but again and again elsewhere in her writings. She will, for example, open a chapter of *Poganuc People* with the statement that "Zeph Higgins was a good Jew." This does not mean that the pious Connecticut farmer was literally of Jewish blood, but simply that he tried to conform to the New England version of the Jewish code. "Zephaniah Pennel," she writes, in *The Pearl of Orr's Island,* "was what might be called a Hebrew of the Hebrews. New England, in her earlier days, founding her institutions on the Hebrew Scriptures, bred better Jews than Moses could, because she read Moses with the amendments of Christ. The state of society in some of the districts of Maine, in these days, much resembled in its spirit that which Moses laboured to produce in ruder ages. It was entirely democratic, simple, grave, hearty and sincere—solemn and religious in its daily tone, and yet, as to all material good, full of wholesome thrift and prosperity." And again, in *Old Town Folks* : "I think no New Englander, brought up under the régime established by the Puritans, could really estimate how much of himself had actually been formed by this constant face-to-face intimacy with Hebrew literature. . . . My grandfather [at family prayers] always prayed standing, and the image of his mild, silvery head, leaning over the top of the high-backed chair, always rises before me as I think of early days. There was no great warmth or fervour in those daily exercises, but rather a serious and decorous propriety. They were Hebraistic in their form; they spoke of Zion and Jerusalem, of the God of Israel, the God of Jacob, as much as if my grandfather had been a veritable Jew; and except for the closing phrase, 'for the sake of Thy Son, our Saviour,' might all have been uttered in Palestine by a well-trained Jew in the time of David." Now, Calvin Stowe, in his Hebraic studies, went on from the Bible to the Talmud, and he prepared a pioneering study of this later difficult work, in which Harriet attempted in vain to interest the *Atlantic Monthly*. He allowed his beard and his hair to grow and wore habitually a rabbinical skull-cap, and, with his spectacles, he presents in his photographs an appearance that would have adorned any synagogue. He liked to pose with a New Testament—in some curious unbooklike form, perhaps masquerading as a Torah scroll—held up before him like Moses' Tablets. His wife was in the habit of referring to him as "my old rabbi" or simply "Old Rab." It may be that, in the case of Calvin Stowe, his Judaizing was a parallel development to that which eventually led Harriet to become an Episcopalian. Harriet had arrived by that time at a full and outspoken revolt against the Calvinist doctrines of Original Sin and salvation through Election; and it may be that Calvin, in a quieter way—he had to teach in Calvinist seminaries —was exemplifying a similar tendency. In Judaism, the Protestant of the Puritan tradition finds the spiritual austerity he already knows, but not bedevilled—the word is exact—by the fear of a despotic Deity who seems to favour or condemn by whim. The Jewish God may be retributory and terrible but he is not preoccupied with torment, nor a perpetrator of nasty surprises as the Calvinist God was.

The most extreme case, however, of an atavistic obsession with the Jews on the part of a well-educated New Englander is that of James Russell Lowell. His mania on this subject is mentioned, in a letter to Charles Eliot Norton, by his English friend Leslie Stephen. "He was so delighted," says Stephen, "with his ingenuity in discovering that everybody was in some way descended from the Jews because he had some Jewish feature, or a Jewish name, or a Gentile name such as the Jews were in the habit of assuming, or because he was connected with one of the departments of business or the geographical regions in which Jews are generally to be found, that it was scarcely possible to mention any distinguished man who could not be conclusively proved to be connected with the chosen race. The logic sometimes seemed to his hearers to have trifling defects; but that was all the greater proof of a sagacity which could dispense with strict methods of proof. To say the truth, this was the only subject upon which I could conceive Lowell approaching within measurable distance of boring." And an anonymous reporter, in the *Atlantic Monthly,* of "Conversations with Mr. Lowell"—quoted in the biography of Lowell by Horace Elisha Scudder—describes in detail such a disquisition.

"At the mention of some medieval Jew," he says, "Lowell at once began to talk of the Jews, a subject which turned out to be almost a monomania with him. He detected a Jew in every hiding place and under every disguise, even when the fugitive had no suspicion of himself. To begin with nomenclature : all persons named for countries or towns are Jews; all with fantastic, compound names, such as Lilienthal, Morgenroth; all with names derived from colours, ·trades, animals, vegetables, minerals; all with Biblical names, except Puritan first names; all patronymics ending in *son, sohn, sen,* or any other versions; all Russels, originally so called from red-haired Israelites; all Walters, by long-descended derivation from wolves and foxes in some ancient tongue; the Caecilii, therefore Cecilia Metella, no doubt St. Cecilia, too, consequently the Cecils, including Lord Burleigh and Lord Salisbury; he cited some old chronicle in which he had cornered one Robert de Caecilia and exposed him as an English Jew. He gave examples and instances of these various classes with amazing readiness and precision, but I will not pretend that I have set down even these correctly. Of course there was Jewish blood in many royal houses and in most noble ones, notably in Spain. In short, it appeared that this insidious race had penetrated and permeated the human family more universally than any other influence except original sin. He spoke of their talent and versatility, and of the numbers who had been illustrious in literature, the learned professions, art, science, and even war, until by degrees, from being shut out of society and every honourable and desirable pursuit they had gained the prominent positions everywhere.

"Then he began his classifications again : all bankers were Jews, likewise brokers, most of the great financiers—and that was to be expected; the majority of barons, also baronets; they had got possession of the press, they were getting into politics; they had forced their entrance into the army and navy; they had made their way into the cabinets of Europe and become prime ministers; they had slipped into diplomacy and become ambassadors. But a short time ago they were packed into the Ghetto : and now they inhabited palaces, the most aristocratic quarters, and were members of the most exclusive clubs. A few years ago they could not own land; they were acquiring it by purchase and mortgage in every part of Europe, and buying so many old estates in England that they owned the larger part of several counties.

"Mr. Lowell said more, much more, to illustrate the ubiquity, the universal ability of the Hebrew, and gave examples and statistics for every statement, however astonishing, drawn from his inexhaustible information. He was conscious of the sort of infatuation which possessed him, and his dissertation alternated between earnestness and drollery; but whenever a burst of laughter greeted some new development of his theme, although he joined in it, he immediately returned to the charge with abundant proof of his paradoxes. Finally he came to a stop, but not to a conclusion, and as no one else spoke, I said, 'And when the Jews have got absolute control of finance, the army and navy, the press, diplomacy, society, titles, the government, and the earth's surface, what do you suppose they will do with them and with us?' 'That,' he answered, turning towards me, and in a whisper audible to the whole table, 'that is the question which will eventually drive me mad.' "

Though Lowell admired the Jews, he conceived them as a power so formidable that they seemed on the verge of becoming a menace. In this vision of a world run entirely by Jews there is something of morbid suspicion, something of the state of mind that leads people to believe in the *Protocols of Zion,* in a Jewish international conspiracy to dominate the civilized world.

But, before trying to get to the sources from which this delusion springs, let me give another example of New England Pan-Judaic doctrine. It might be thought that Barrett Wendell of Harvard was the perfect type of old-fashioned snob in regard to every kind of American not of strictly Anglo-Saxon origins, yet we find him —on October 18th, 1891—writing to his father as follows: "I heard a queer theory the other day about the Yankee Puritans, whose religious views were so strongly Hebraic. They came chiefly, it seems, from Norfolk and Lincolnshire. These counties, some two or three centuries before the Reformation, had been the chief strongholds of the English Jews, who were finally expelled from the kingdom by one of the Plantagenet kings. At the time of the expulsion, many changed their faith and remained to be absorbed in the native population. It is wholly possible, then, that the Yankee Puritan, with all his Old Testament feeling, was really, without knowing it, largely Jewish in blood. There is in the Yankee nature much that would give colour to the theory; but of course it is very far from being a proved fact. . . ." Is there any actual evidence for this or have we here simply a recrudescence of the Judaizing tendency of the Puritan?

I have noted that Lowell's prophecy of a universal Jewish dominance seems to skirt the state of mind of those who believe in the *Protocols of Zion*. It is possible to cite examples of a glorification of the Jews that has passed suddenly into a neurotic anti-Semitism. Such an example was the late John Jay Chapman. He was a mixture of New York and New England, but the New England strain in him was very strong. His grandmother had been a lieutenant of William Lloyd Garrison, whom (Garrison) Chapman very much admired and about whom he wrote a book. Especially in this connection his relations with the Jews are significant. "There is a depth of human feeling in the Jew," he wrote in a memorandum of 1897, "that no other race ever possessed. We do no more than imitate it and follow it. David, for instance, and his conduct about Uriah's wife and the child that died—and Absalom—and Jonathan. Compare the Greek—the Chinese, the Roman. These Jews are more human than any other men. It is the cause of the spread of their religion—for we are all adopted into Judah. The heart of the world is Jewish. There is the same spirit in the Old Testament as in the New. What monstrous perversion—that we should worship their God and despise themselves! We admire the Pyramids and the Egyptians, but the history of the Jews is the most remarkable, the most notable thing, on the globe.

Their sacred books and chronicles and traditions and history make the annals of every other nation mere rubbish—and I feel this same power in the Jews I know. They are the most humane and the strongest people morally, mentally and physically. They persist. I'm glad I'm a Jew. I believe that's the reason why this paper-faced civilization impresses me so little. Take Habakkuk," etc. (It was true that Chapman looked rather Jewish, and he wore an impressive beard in a period when beards had ceased to be fashionable; but neither Chapman himself in his memoirs, nor his biographer, Mr. M. A. deWolfe Howe, records that he had Jewish blood.)

This pro-Semitism was unquestionably to some extent due to Chapman's political dependence on a devoted Jewish friend, Mr. Isaac H. Klein of New York, who worked with him in his efforts at reform. "The Jews have in my experience," he writes in a letter dated from Wall Street, a little later in 1897, "more faith than the Christians. They have clever heads, better hearts and more belief in the power of good every way. They gave to the world all the religion it has got and are themselves the most religious people in it. I work with them day and night and most of the time is spent in prying up some Christian to do a half day's work."

But between the eighteen nineties and the nineteen twenties, Chapman's attitude towards the Jews underwent an astonishing change. One gets the impression from a letter, written from Atlantic City, of December 1919, that his disillusion may have begun with the spectacle of crowds of vacationing Jews who did not strike him as being the equals of Habakkuk and Isaac Klein : "They are uncritical," he now writes. "Life is a simple matter to them : a bank account and the larder. No, they will never rule the world. They are too easily deflected—absorbed and satisfied. It is foolish to rule the world and the Jew knows it. They are crumbling material for the hands of their leaders, and ropes of sand. They have too much sense—and will go for the glittering garments and not murder Progress. They strike me as an inferior race, in spite of their great advantages. . . . But to return to the Jews, my long acquaintance with Klein and his club makes me at home with them—but I'm glad I haven't *more* Jewish blood in me than I have. I don't want any more. These people don't know anything. They have no religion, no customs except eating and drinking."

Note here again the spectre of Jewish power. As Chapman watches a crowd of Jews behaving in a perfectly natural way, he concludes that they will not "rule the world." Why should he have expected them to?—and why should he be surprised that these citizens from New York and Philadelphia show an interest in their larders and their bank accounts? Do Americans of other stocks not give evidence of similar interests? Later on, he went even further and began to link the Jews with the Catholics in his attacks on the Catholic church. He actually got to the point of publishing in an organ of the Ku Klux Klan—the *National Kourier* of May 20th, 1925—the following queer anti-Semitic sonnet:

CAPE COD, ROME AND JERUSALEM

How restful is it to survey the sea
From some low, windswept, silvery, sandy dune,
And watch the eternal climbing of the moon
Full-orbed, above the shore's complacency;
Wondering the while if Asian plains there be,
Or rock-walled valleys, never shined upon—
Save by the perpendicular sun at noon—
So safe, so guarded, so remote as we.

But see, a sail!—nay more—from every land
They cloud the ocean, convoyed by a crew
Of Master Pirates who have work in hand:
Old Europe's nation-wreckers heave in view!
And lo, to aid them, on our margin stand
Our citizens—the Jesuit and the Jew.

There is, I think, involved in Chapman's case, as perhaps in Lowell's also, a special relation to the Judaic element in the Puritan New England tradition. This tradition came to life again —after a partial eclipse during the early eighteen hundreds—in the Abolitionist crusade against slavery that inspired so much of the ardour of the Federal forces in the Civil War. *The Battle Hymn of the Republic* comes straight out of the Biblical Prophets, and the Jehovah of the Old Testament takes the field again at the head of the Federal armies. In the period before the war, Lowell had been stirred by this fervour—under the influence, it is said, of his first wife—and had worked for the Abolitionist cause; John Jay Chapman, who was proud of his grandmother, and had relived the Abolitionist movement in writing his book about Garrison, had once travelled to a Pennsylvanian town where a Negro had been burned alive to hold an expiatory meeting—a meeting at which he was the only speaker and to which only two people came. Both Lowell and Chapman, in their later years, more or less dropped crusading, somewhat lapsed in their faith. The former, ambassador to the Court of St. James, became an official figure; the latter, having married a well-to-do wife, became the proprietor of a country estate and a somewhat petulant critic of everyone in literature and politics who was playing a more active part than he. Both, perhaps, had a bad conscience. In Lowell's case he seems half to hope, half to fear, that the Puritan-Jewish Jehovah is going to take over the world; in Chapman's case, he seems—not admitting it—to be gnawed by a sense of guilt towards the moral inspiration of the Jews in which he has felt he shared : he accuses lest he stand condemned.

But there is something else, too, in this curious shift from a faith in the Jews to a fear of them. The basic thing here, I believe, is that the Jews have been all too successful in convincing the rest of the world of their privileged relations with God. They have made it all too easy for visionary people—that is, people like themselves—to assume that there is something supernatural about them. What Chapman, who has idealized the Jews on the evidence of the Bible and of his friend Mr. Klein, was so startled one day to realize, on the boardwalk at Atlantic City, was that German or Russian or Polish or Lithuanian Jewish Americans were human beings like everyone else. And yet for a certain type of mind— the apocalyptical kind—it is difficult to accept this conclusion. For such a mind, an awe of the Jews persists but it takes on a different aspect. It may turn to the extreme anti-Semitism of Hitler and Henry Ford—both idealistic cranks—which, as Waldo Frank has said in his study *The Jew in Our Day*, is a department of demonology. Or it may merely—as in Lowell's case—survive as a superstition, an uneasiness in the presence of something unknown, an uncomfortable apprehension. These people, unique in their cohesiveness, their inbreeding, their self-isolation, so impressive in their sureness of their contact with God, is there not something queer about them? Do they not possess special powers? May they not be masters of a magic that enables them to intrigue against us, to demoralize, subvert, destroy us? Nor is it, I think, out of the question that we ourselves, deep in our "psyches," may consider it correct that we should thus be destroyed in punishment for our own apostasy, our apostasy towards, precisely, the Jewish God— that apostasy of which the two Testaments have combined, at the basis of our moral training, to implant in us the sense of danger?

An odd non-American example of this tendency to credit the Jews with supernatural powers is to be found in the novels of George du Maurier. I have not been able to discover in any of the biographical material about him that du Maurier himself had a Jewish strain; but in each of his three novels a rather unexpected Jewish theme plays a more or less important rôle. In the first of these, *Peter Ibbetson,* we are told of the mother of Colonel Ibbetson that she "had been the only child and heiress of an immensely rich pawnbroker, by name Mendoza; a Portuguese Jew, with a dash of coloured blood in his veins, besides, it was said." But Peter himself is a nephew of the Colonel's on the latter's *paternal* side, and the Jewish character here is the villain. In *The Martian,* on the other hand, the third of the series, a woman with Jewish blood is the heroine. We are told of Leah Gibson that "her mother . . . was a Spanish Jewess—a most magnificent and beautiful old person in splendid attire, tall and straight, with white hair and thick black eyebrows, and large eyes as black as night. In Leah the high Sephardic Jewish type was more marked than in Mrs. Gibson. . . . It is a type that sometimes, just now and again, can be so pathetically noble and beautiful in a woman, so suggestive of chastity and the most passionate love combined—love conjugal and filial and maternal—love that implies all the big practical obligations and responsibilities of human life, that the mere term 'Jewess' (and especially its French equivalent) brings to my mind some vague, mysterious, exotically poetic image of all I love best in woman." But in the intermediate *Trilby,* du Maurier's conception of the Jew is developed in a major and a very strange way. We are told, in the first place, of Little Billee, one of the three British art students in Paris about whom the story centres, that "in his winning and handsome face there was just a faint suggestion of some possible very remote Jewish ancestor—just a tinge of that strong, sturdy, irrepressible, indomitable, indelible blood which is of such priceless value in diluted homoeopathic doses, like the dry white Spanish wine called Montijo, which is not meant to be taken pure; but without a judicious admixture of which no sherry can go round the world and keep its flavour intact; or like the famous bull-dog strain, which is not beautiful in itself; and yet just for lacking a little of the same no greyhound can ever be a champion." Little Billee is thus the only one of the three companions who is shown to possess any genuine talent. But the great Jewish character in *Trilby* is, of course, the German-Jewish Svengali : the fabulous musician who cannot sing but who, by hypnotizing the tone-deaf Trilby and exploiting her wonderful voice, makes of her a great artist. Svengali, in other connections, is always represented as everything that these gentlemanly Britishers most abhor : he is dirty, insulting, boastful, mendacious, malicious, quarrelsome; they have constantly to put him in his place. Yet Trilby, in spite of her voice, has not only no ear whatever for music, no range of emotion or expression which would be adequate, even if she had one, to achieve the astounding effects which Svengali is able to teach her by turning her into a simple automaton. The concert— described at great length—at which Trilby so triumphantly sings, is "the apotheosis of voice and virtuosity"; she sounds like a combination of Adelina Patti and Yvette Guilbert. Yet—except for the voice itself—the whole thing is an emanation of Svengali's musical soul; and if this is true, the horrid Svengali must have, after all, as Bernard Shaw says, "better grounds for [his] egotism than anybody else in the book except Little Billee and Trilby." But from whence does all this subtlety and innocence, this tenderness and joy and sorrow, arise in the Svengali we know? There is no explanation of this : the character, in human terms, is not in any deep sense created. What is really behind Svengali is the notion, again, that the Jew, even in his squalidest form, is a mouthpiece of our Judaico-Christian God, whose voice he has, in this case, transferred, ventriloquially, to the throat of Trilby. There is always in these novels of du Maurier's—binational, bilingual as he was—a certain light playing-off of French civilization against English; but the picture is further complicated—it is one of the things that make them interesting—by this dual rôle of the Jew, who appears —in Colonel Ibbetson, Svengali in his ordinary relations—now as a malignant devil, whose malignancy is hardly accounted for; now —in Leah, Little Billee and the Svengali who animates Trilby— as a spirit from an alien world who carries with it an uncanny prestige, who may speak in a divine tongue.

In the meantime, for the Jew—or for many Jews—it must become almost as embarrassing to be taken for a Hebrew prophet on confidential terms with God as for a diabolical demiurge who is out to "murder Progress"—whatever Chapman meant by that. I remember a clear illustration of this in a story told of himself by Dr. Paul Tillich of Union Theological Seminary in a discussion after one of his seminars. Dr. Tillich explained that he had never at first approved of the Zionist movement. He had thought it a good thing that a group—the Jews—should survive in the modern world to represent a religious faith independent of patriotism, whose kingdom—since they had no country—could not be of this world. But it was then pointed out to him by a Jewish friend that he was being quite unfair to "the petty bourgeois Cohens and Levis," who could hardly be expected to be Moseses and Isaiahs, and who ought not to be restricted to the status of aliens in countries in which they were still not accepted on quite the same basis as other natives and which were liable to anti-Semitic panics. Dr. Tillich was so struck by the justice of this that he at once joined a Zionist organization.

.   .   .

To look into, to contemplate Judaism after living with Christianity is to feel at first a certain emptiness. But it is something of a relief, also, to get rid of the Christian mythology. The half-human figure of the Saviour is likely to introduce a disquieting personal element. The Christian must refer himself to Jesus. What would Jesus have done? What does He want me to do? How should a Christian behave? Or—in the case of a more fervent person—he may go further and identify himself with Christ : struggle with temptations, endure ordeals, offer himself to martyr-doms. There is always an emotional relationship to another half-human being, and—since this being is the Son of God—through him, to a Heavenly Father who is bound to be more or less an-thropomorphic. But the God of the Jews is remote : one cannot speak or write his name. He has no go-between but the prophets, and these are human beings, whose words one uses in praying but to whom one does not pray. In the Calvinist church, to be sure, Jesus Christ played a minor rôle, could hardly, in some cases, be said to figure; yet, in contrast to this kind of "Christianity," too, the theology of Judaism affords a relief : no worry about being Elected, no preoccupation with Hell.

Thus if the outlook of Judaism seems somewhat bleak, if its observances—to a non-Jew—mean little, some contact with it is none the less bracing. We are living with God in an empty room—in a room without pictures : the synagogue, where the only things displayed on the walls are words. These words declare the power of the spirit, the authority of the moral sense. The source of this power and authority gains dignity from not being seen, from not being given a name, from being communicated with—not through the bread and wine of Christ's flesh and blood—but only through thought and prayer. There is only the conviction of its eternal reality, and sometimes of its actual presence.

The Messiah at the Seder

A middle-aged group of old friends had gathered for the Passover Seder. The host was the son of a rabbi and had studied for
ordination in his youth at the Jewish Theological Seminary, but
he now worked on the staff of a Jewish magazine. The men
guests were a professor of Hebrew; a Viennese psychoanalyst; and
a formerly active Marxist, who had fallen back on editing an
encyclopedia. The scholar and the Marxist were accompanied by
their wives, but the analyst was at present estranged from his,
and the hostess's sister made the fourth woman : a handsome
vivacious girl, somewhat younger than the others and unmarried.
The Seder is designed to be a family affair, but it happened, on
this occasion, that no children took part in the ceremony. Those
of the host and hostess were under ten and had been put to bed;
the Marxist and his wife were childless; the Hebraist's sons were
married and living in other cities; and the adolescent son of the
analyst had been carried off by his mother. Though parts of the
Seder service are especially intended for children and cannot have
their full effect without them, it was perhaps on this occasion, in
view of what happened, just as well that there were no children
present.

None of the company in their ordinary lives conformed with
the observances of Orthodox Judaism. Only the professor and his
wife practised a kosher cuisine, and the dinner tonight was not
kosher. But most had had some schooling in Hebrew, and all had
been brought up in the old way. All enjoyed celebrating this
festival, which strengthened the family unit, reinforced the ties
among friends, affirmed the solidarity of the Jewish people. In all
this it differed much from any feast-day or holy service of their
neighbours, either Catholic or Protestant—for it combined a family
party like Christmas dinner with a ritual of resurrection that re-

sembled an Easter Mass. The men, although mostly beardless—
the professor was the only exception—all wore, for the special
occasion, the close-fitting round black caps that made them at
home in the Jewish world, and all read aloud from the Haggadah,
the traditional Hebrew text, of which each had a copy before him.
Two of the wives, who knew no Hebrew, abstained, but the hostess
and her sister participated, since they, also, were the children of a
rabbi. This text, in its lyrical eloquence, its variety and its flexibility—for it ranges from rhymes for the children to exalted psalms
in praise of God—its invocation of sanctions that dignify the
meagrest meal, its exultant reawakening of the Jewish sense of
consecration, which springs to life among the human actualities of
the homeliest Jewish family, was felt by them all as a spell that
involved the long dinner table, white-naperied, gleaming with wine
glasses and studded with the red and yellow bottles that contained
the ceremonial wine; and connected them—there in a modern
apartment of uptown West-Side New York—with the legendary
past of their people, or rather, with something that was scarcely
for them either legendary or even past, since it still lived among
them there, and that was not what had happened but what they
were living. For, dealing with events that—in terms of our time—
must have occurred four thousand years before, composed now in
Biblical Hebrew, now in Aramaic of the Exile, now in the dialect
of the Talmud, now borrowed from the hymns of the Middle Ages,
blending Provence with Babylon, the Haggadah is timeless:
excreted, accreted, as it is, by the anonymous processes of centuries,
it concentrates in one vibrant poem the despairs and the hopes of
millennia.

The celebrants at a Seder are supposed to recline in the manner
of a Roman banquet, but today this is only approximated by a
cushion or two behind the host. The ritual this evening, to be
sure, was a little cavalierly treated, but it is one of the charms of
the Seder that it combines the petition and the paean to God with
a comfortable informality, and they had not had tonight any
intimation that something of importance was due to occur. The
Hebrew had been fluent, the singing quite good. Almost all knew
the music from childhood, and they could pick up the ancient
cadences as readily as the words of a prayer. The sister-in-law of

the host had a fresh and silvery voice that caressed and enlivened the spirit. The host had blessed the banquet, and the first cup of wine had been drunk. He had rinsed his hands in a fingerbowl, and the Karpas had been passed around : sprigs of parsley dipped in salt water that represented the bunches of hyssop, dipped in the blood of the Paschal lamb, which, on the eve of the Exodus from Egypt, were used to mark the doorways of the Israelites, so that the Angel of Death would pass by them. The host had then broken the middle Mazzah, a brittle unleavened biscuit, and had stuck away a piece of it in the cushions behind him, and, with the aid of his neighbours on either side, he had held up before him the tray on which lay the egg and the shankbone of lamb : "This is the bread of affliction that our fathers ate in the land of Egypt. All who are hungered—let them come to eat; all who are needy—let them come and celebrate the Passover. Now we are here, but next year may we be in the land of Israel! Now we are slaves, but next year may we be free men!"

The four questions were now asked—failing a child, by the youngest person present, who was the sister-in-law of the host : "How is this night different from other nights?" in respect to the four points of the ritual of dining—which leads to the announcement of the coming-forth from Egypt, with its pleasant little digression, the story of the five rabbis who sat up so late at night telling of this event that their pupils, the next morning, had found them still talking and had to summon them to morning prayer. Then the episode of the four sons : the clever one, the rude one, the simple one and the one who is too young to know how to ask—to each of whom, in suitable terms, the meaning of the ritual must be explained. The goblets had been raised and put down, the Mazzoth covered and uncovered : the promise made to Abraham, the bondage in Egypt, the outcry to God, who remembers—"And God saw the children of Israel, and God knew"; the enumeration of the plagues of Israel, with a drop of wine spilled for each, and the summing-up of these by the strange mnemonic device—"the scorpion stung the uncle"—invented by the Rabbi Judah.

Then, the hymn of Thanksgiving to God, with its trumpet-like refrain "Deyéynu!" which raises the note of rejoicing at His benefits beyond hoping to Israel. They had eaten of the Mazzah, in remembrance of the bread, baked in haste without leaven, which their fathers had brought with them out of Egypt; of the Bitter Herb—a dish of horseradish—in memory of the bitterness of their misery in bondage, but sweetened by the Haroseth, a relish of chopped apples, raisins and almonds, which stands for the mortar that the Israelite captives were forced to mix for their masters, and which has several other meanings as well. They had drunk the second glass of wine. They had rinsed their fingers in bowls and had listened to the benediction.

The hostess and her sister now brought on the dinner, for which each of the families present had provided one of the dishes. It began with the customary hard-boiled egg served in a bowl of salt water—at once a tongue-whetting hors-d'oeuvre and a reminder, again, of affliction, and went on to a main course of chicken, a permissible substitute for the Paschal lamb. They drank freely now, during dinner, in a non-ritualistic way, and the talk became very lively. They mingled discussion of current events with some effort to keep up the tradition of interpreting and analysing the service. They criticized the Jewish press, condemning it in all its departments and not sparing the magazine of which their host was an editor. The analyst had some new jokes about Israel. The professor spoke with sharp severity of an eminent Jewish scholar, to whom he referred as "a *yeshiva bochar*." The sister-in-law, next to the analyst, allowed herself to play up to him with dark sidelong glances, and even to propound to him one of her dreams, of which he gave her a frivolous interpretation : "Right off the bat, I'd say that the big black dog was McCarthy, for whom you feel an unconfessed admiration." The wife of the Marxist at one point inquired the origin of the word *Afikoman,* applied to the section of Mazzah that the host hides behind his cushion, and it was explained to her that, according to the Mishnah, this was derived from one or the other of two Greek words meaning, respectively, a festal song and an after-dinner dessert. This piece of unleavened biscuit is eaten at the end of the banquet, and figures as a symbolic substitute for any further form of entertainment. It is forbidden, when the Seder is over, to go on to any other affair.

Now the ritual had been resumed with the comedy of this Afikoman. The fragment of Mazzah is supposed to have been stolen by the youngest child present from the cushions where the father has hidden it, and to be ransomed, at this point in the ceremony, for the minimum price of a quarter. But this evening the part had been played by the handsome sister-in-law, who took an audacious line. When the host had reached for the Afikoman, and had exclaimed that it must have been stolen, and when the sister-in-law had produced it and had been asked what she would take to give it back, she had answered that he could give her in return for it that map of the Middle East, with the names all printed in Hebrew, that he had been showing them before dinner. He managed not to commit himself clearly to this, but she handed him back the Afikoman, which was now broken into bits and handed around the table. Everybody ate a piece. To eat a large amount of the Afikoman is said to prolong life, but though some remembered this, no one did more than nibble. Now the invocation of blessings began again, and the third ritual cup was drunk. "Pour out Thy wrath," they chanted, "upon the heathen that have not known Thee, and upon the kingdoms that have not called upon Thy name : for they have devoured Jacob and have laid waste his dwelling-place. Pour out upon them Thine indignation and let Thy fierce anger overtake them. Pursue them in wrath and destroy them from under the heavens of the Lord."

At this point, the host left the table, went into the hall of the apartment and opened the door into the outer hall. This was done for the Prophet Elijah, who circulates among his people and is present on certain occasions. A chair is set out for Elijah at the ceremony of circumcision, and is left there for three days, till the child is over the worst. At Passover, however he had never yet come; he was expected—when the hour should arrive—to announce the Messiah's advent. When the fourth cup of wine was poured, a special silver goblet was also filled and set apart on the table for the prophet. This was called the Cup of the Redemption, because it was prepared for the moment when Israel should be redeemed and led back by the Messiah to its home in Jerusalem.

The host had regained his place, and they were proceeding with the chanting of the Haggadah when the professor of Hebrew, who was opposite the door, became aware that someone had entered and, looking up, beheld a tall old man whom he took at first for an Arab. This visitor was dressed in a kind of white cloak that had long sleeves and came to his knees, and a headdress that was a large folded napkin with the ends crossed under his chin and tied on with a heavy cord. He wore sandals, and his bare legs were sinewy, sunburnt and hairy. His face was as dark as dark leather, and his coarse hair and beard were untrimmed. The professor stopped reading, and everybody looked up. The old man stopped just inside the door and, throwing back his head, began to declaim in a voice somewhat high and nasal and with heavily marked rhythms that gave almost the effect of singing. It seemed to them that they recognized the language as Hebrew, but they could not make out what he was saying. The guttural sounds suggested to some that the language he was speaking was Arabic. It was only the concluding sentence that they definitely understood, for it contained two of the most familiar Hebrew nouns : "Peace will now come over the whole earth !"

"What a hideous travesty," the Hebraist thought, "of the ancient pronunciation !" He had read that among the Caucasian Jews it was a custom for some young man of the family to appear as a pilgrim come back from Jerusalem to tell them that the Redemption would not now be long, and he was not able to make up his mind whether one ought to resent a prank and say to the visitor, "That isn't funny !" or to accept it as a possible feature of the Seder. In any case, it was up to their host. He remembered that the host's parents came from Southern Russia. He might perhaps himself have arranged this.

But now a second visitor presented himself, putting his hand on the old man's shoulder and making him stand aside. This was a lean but strong-shouldered little man, wearing the black Jewish skull-cap and dressed in a blue double-breasted suit, who had high cheekbones, a vehement chin and a fine sharply beak-like nose. His pale complexion was flushed, and a look of obsessive intensity was sparked from his myopic green eyes, but when he spoke, it seemed plain that he was forcing himself to avoid an exalted tone.

"I don't know whether you got what he said," he began. "This is the Prophet Elijah. He's just announced my coming."

"And who are you ?" demanded the scholar.

"The Messiah, believe it or not. You're sceptical. I think that we can soon convince you."

"I should question that," the Hebraist retorted, with a disagreeable smile. "Don't you know that the Messiah does not arrive till three days after Elijah's announcement?"

"If you really want to convince us," said the head of the house, smiling with more amiability, "you'll have to give us the Seven Miracles."

"Talmudic folk-lore!" said the visitor. "We don't need to bother with that. The more we speed things up the better. But you're worrying about credentials. Well, first of all, I'll give you my story." It was evident that he had it on tap. "There was nothing at all out of the ordinary about my early boyhood. I was a run-of-the-mill child prodigy. My father made middle-class furniture in Brooklyn. He was successful but he hadn't had an education, and he wanted to make up for it through me. I had mastered calculus at eight—I played the cello and composed at ten. I graduated from college at thirteen and did advanced work in nuclear physics. But the day I became Bar Mitzvah—the night after I'd been at the synagogue—I was lying in bed—awake—and I heard a voice that called me : 'Shemuel! Shemuel!'—my name is Samuel—and I answered, *'Hineyni.'* The Lord first spoke to me then. He told me I was to lead my people back to the land of Israel. Then, on May 14th, 1947—just seven years later, and forty-seven, notice—I heard the Voice speak to me again. It told me that a year from that day the big ingathering would have begun and Israel would be proclaimed a free and independent state. I was just twenty-one at the time, and I was working on Long Island on the atom bomb. The Lord, blessed be He, told me again that I was to lead back my people to Jerusalem—that the nations were to be governed from Zion and peace was to come to the world—just what Elijah was telling you. I threw up my job then and fasted, and then—when I was weak with hunger—I was constantly in touch with the Lord. He told me to work for an organization that was raising money for Israel. That went on for seven years. Then came the final call—last year—the Eve of Passover and the day when Maimonides was born : Nisan 14—May 14th, Nisan 14, and both double seven—it bridges the gap between the calendars—and that gave me conclusive proof that it wasn't an hallucination. Note also that, according to our calendar, it was the year 5714—seven and double seven. I was told that a year from that Passover the time would have come to save Israel and for Israel to save the world. I've been working on the project all year. In a sense, we worked it out together. But it's only the upshot that interests you, and that is that the Redemption is at hand—you must get transportation for Israel at the earliest possible moment. The arrangements haven't all been made yet, but there'll be extra planes and boats put on—about that I can be quite positive. Well, there you have the story, and if you don't accept me now, you will a little later on, when the Power behind me begins to work. In the meantime, just to look at our friend here" —and he put his hand on Elijah's shoulder—"ought to say something to you."

The old man, while the Messiah was talking, had been looking around the room with his dark and transfixing eyes, trained like guns from beneath shaggy eyebrows and flanking a magistral Hebraic nose. The young man quickly slipped aside and took down from the dining-room walls a Picasso and a Modigliani, which he set on the floor behind him, with their faces against the wall.

"I didn't want him to be smashing them," he said. "He might think they were Baal or something."

The host's handsome sister-in-law began to feel rather self-conscious. She was wearing large dangling earrings and a bright red damask gown. Personal adornments, of course, were permitted by the Talmud, if properly made, and she remembered that there were earrings in the Bible, but Elijah did look terribly austere. Even if he were not Elijah, but just some insane fanatic, one would hate to be blasted by him! She dropped her eyes to the table: had she really been thinking, she wondered, about having an affair with the analyst?

"Won't you please sit down," said the host. He brought in chairs from another room, and his wife made places for the visitors. He was by no means persuaded of their authenticity but—well versed in rabbinical lore—it came back to him, as the old prophet took his seat and sat erect with one hand on his knee and the other in a kind of pocket that was formed at his breast by a fold of his cloak, that the pious Rabbi Judah of Regensburg had once, at a certain circumcision, been able to perceive that Elijah was absent from his appointed chair, which had augured—it proved, truly—that the child would abandon the Jewish faith. He could not, in any case, but be glad that the visitors had found them at their correct observances. His wife was a little embarrassed at having chicken instead of lamb, and she had hesitated about offering them the non-kosher dinner, but the host now invited them to eat.

"Not for me," said the young man, "but the Prophet might like a snack. This is the first time he's come to a Sedar, and I think he'd enjoy eating something." A brief question in Hebrew brought a nod from the old man. The hostess went to heat up something, and in the meantime the formidable visitor, casting his eye about, identified the goblet set out for him and drained it at a single draught. This a little astonished the host, for the time had not yet come in the ceremony when the fourth cup of wine is drunk; but he remembered from II Kings, xxiii. 22, that between the days of the Judges and the very late reign of Josiah no Passover had ever been celebrated, so that Elijah would not know the ceremony—although wasn't the ritual itself even much later than that?—the four cups of wine, he thought, had been mentioned first in the Mishnah.

But such questions were blurring in his mind. Had he drunk too many glasses at dinner, besides the ceremonial three? Or was he actually feeling the Power of which the young man had spoken, the Power behind him and Elijah? Did they not both have a radiance about them?—did they not, together, create a field in which was intensified and rarefied the yellow electric light? From the moment they sat down at the table, it was impossible not to treat them with deference. They brought silence, imposed themselves. It seemed most difficult to ask them questions. Yet the thought had dawned in every mind that the self-presented Messiah was one of those forced infant prodigies who break down from precocious effort. Had not the nocturnal call of the Lord been suggested by his name, Samuel? The analyst had been watching him shrewdly, had noted that he had left off the glasses without which he was nearly blind in order to make a better impression, that he had had some experience in public speaking, and, physically so unprepossessing, had acquired certain tricks of tone to propitiate and win an audience. Yet the gaze now laid bare by the discarding of his lenses had about it something fervent and gentle that first touched one, then evoked respect; his passion, so determinedly repressed, as he told about his call from God, seemed to burn away a commonness of accent.

The analyst itched to examine him, to lay bare the links of suggestion, the mechanism of instinct and impasse which had braced him to the strength of his delusion. He himself had been very careful not to push his own son too much; but then his wife, once a patient of his, had messed the relationship up, and might, he feared, make the boy another neurotic. The childless wife of the scholar was wondering whether her husband, a despotic and pitiless pedant, would have tried to turn their boy into a prodigy, and, having sometimes indulged herself in the dream of an ambitious son who would become a big business executive, was just as glad she had not had to risk it. The hostess, bringing on the hot plate, had asked the young man again whether he was sure he would not have a snack—she could see he was starving himself. "There's no fasting on Passover," she smiled. But he dismissed it with a negative nod. She thought of her own fat-cheeked children : she would never, she told herself, allow them to go rocketing out of her orbit; but maybe his parents were dead !

A constraint fell upon the whole company. The Marxist was the first to break through it. "Let us ask you a practical question :"—he put it to the Messiah as man to man—"Do you expect all the Jews in the world—all the Jews that aren't in Israel already—to emigrate with you there?"

"In the long run, we certainly expect it, but we're not giving everyone the call tonight."

"May I ask what your principle of selection is?"

"Only those that are holding Seders. We figure that we at least have a chance with *them*. They include, of course, a number of non-believers, or people who think they are, but the fact that they celebrate Passover would indicate that their ties with Judaism are not completely severed."

"Will you have the time to call on every Seder—tonight or tomorrow night?"

"I visit many Seders simultaneously. Between 7 a.m. today and 7 tomorrow morning. I am visiting every Seder from Oslo to Valparaiso."

This stopped the questioner for only a second. "How do you manage that?"

"How do Milt Berle and Monsignor Sheen manage to appear at the same time on every TV screen in New York?"

"That's only a projected photograph, but you're present with us here in this room, and you say that you're also present at a number of other Seders."

"That's correct. You can see me here; you can hear me; I can handle those pictures; but all the time my real basic self is at my headquarters on Ninety-Second Street directing the whole thing."

"I see," said the Marxist.

The analyst took it up: "Can you tell us how this is accomplished?"

"You wouldn't be able to grasp it. It hasn't been worked out by man, so the steps would be unintelligible. I don't understand it myself. It's only the Lord, blessed be He, who makes it possible for me to do all this."

Another queer but apposite reference came back into the mind of the host. The learned Lipmann-Mülhausen, in his *Sepher ha-Nizzahon,* had dealt with precisely the problem of the appearance of the Prophet Elijah simultaneously in different places, and had disposed of practical objections in terms of the pervasion of sunlight and the ubiquity of the Angel of Death.

"But supposing," pursued the Marxist, "that your call is successful tonight. There surely isn't room in Israel for all the dispersed Jews holding Seders."

"We won't be confined to the present area."

"How so?"

"Well, just give a thought to those plagues you've been reading about in the Haggadah. You're going to pick up the paper tomorrow and see that all the Arabs are dropping dead."

The Marxist could not help smiling; the Hebrew scholar sneered. The analyst asked a question in his professional matter-of-fact way : "And how will *that* be accomplished? Bacteriological warfare?"

"You're a long distance behind us again. It's done by a simple vibration—but not, in the crude sense, electrical. Don't worry about the humanitarian angle : death is instantaneous."

"You'll have a disposal problem," suggested the Marxist.

"The bodies crumble to dust. They blow away and mix with the sand."

"Will the other countries," the Marxist inquired, "accept Jewish hegemony? If I understand you, that's what you aim at."

"They will see we have the Lord behind us, and our prestige will rapidly increase."

"You're not afraid," the Marxist pressed him, "that pulverizing all the Arabs will create a bad impression?"

"It'll be the most conspicuous miracle since the crossing of the Red Sea. Who cares about Pharaoh's army?"

"I'm interested"—the host changed the subject—"in the theological aspect. Is there to be a Day of the Lord?"

"There is."

"Would you care to develop that subject? Maimonides tells us that the dead are to rise."

"We can't do anything with that at the present time. We've already got enough mixed elements. And even with the formerly Arab areas, we're not able to accommodate everybody—the dead as well as the living."

"What about reward and punishment?" the hostess's sister asked. She had already had two serious love affairs, one with a married man.

"Yes," said the host : "we read in Saadia that everyone will be steeped in a divine fire, and that this fire will shine for the redeemed without burning them, but eternally burn the unredeemed without shining on them."

"Saadia is not the last word. Maimonides is not the last word," the Messiah replied with assurance.

"But there *will* be reward and punishment?"

"Correct. There will be what I have termed an Assize of Exclusion—exclusion on rigorous principles."

"What will happen to the people excluded?"

"Will they be pulverized?" inquired the analyst.

"Only Arabs will be pulverized," the Messiah replied. "Jews who are unredeemed will not be permitted to live in Israel."

"And you," said the analyst quietly, "are to be the judge of Redemption?"

"With the help of the Lord, yes."

"I am wondering," said the host, "how these things are to be decided. If it is a question of observance of the Law, there is nobody in this room who would qualify."

"So far as observances go, we have, of course, adapted ourselves to the modern developments of Judaism. A good many of the observances, as the Name well knows, have long ago outlived their usefulness; some are unscientific. There's no question of discrimination against members of Conservative or Reformed congregations —or even against good Jews who don't go to the Temple at all. But a minimum of observance we do demand—that's why we begin at the Seder. The Commandments, however, are a different matter. That's where we go along with Maimonides. Grave infractions will be hard to outweigh."

"But of course you will have other criteria?" the Marxist asked a little aggressively.

"Of course : our decisions will be made in accordance with a code of morality which has been formulated by strict definitions."

"It hardly seems fair," said the host, "that we shouldn't have been told about this." His wife, the rabbi's daughter, firmly backed him up : "If we've never been told this code, how could we know that we were violating it?" "And they're asking us to go back," thought her sister, still uneasy on the score of the Seventh Commandment, "with the risk of being thrown out !"

"It's based on the Ten Commandments, and it conforms to the best tradition of Judaism. It's an extension of the Commandments themselves. We interpret them in such a way as to take into account the new conditions that have come to prevail since they were first handed down. That's all I can tell you now."

"Couldn't you give us an idea," asked the analyst, "of the way in which this system of interpretation would work in a specific instance?"

"It's useless to discuss it," the Messiah declared. "You'll be able to learn something about it when you see it applied in practice. But actually you'll never be able fully to comprehend it. The wisdom of the Lord, as you know, passes understanding. Even the greatest prophets could not compass all His aims and methods, and even I, who am admitted to His confidence, fall short of the full revelation. I've helped Him to organize the Judgment in an orderly and practical way, but for difficult decisions I must go to Him."

This seemed to arouse the Marxist, who, brusquely, took a bolder line. "You've spoken," he said, "of your training in the mathematical sciences, and also, to some extent, in music. Are we to take it for granted that you're equally at home in all the arts and professions?"

"Potentially, yes; but that's irrelevant. Our judgment in any given case is strictly a moral matter; it doesn't involve the specific skill in which the individual may be proficient."

"I ask because I don't understand how it is possible to judge an individual working in any field without thoroughgoing training in that field, life-long experience of it. Morality that is correct implies correct doctrine. Admittedly, as you were saying, the Torah and the Talmud—including the Commandments—are codes that belong to the earlier phases of social-economic development. They are useless to guide us today among the contradictions of modern society, the mazes of modern politics. And how can social theory, how can political procedure, be judged by a professional physicist? I assume that you are not a Marxist. For a Marxist it would have been quite impossible to work even a day, even an hour, in a laboratory making the bomb!"

"Marx is one of our prophets——"

"Exactly: the greatest of our prophets. But one has to study Marxist theory, to become adept at Marxist practice, in order to know how to discriminate between the true and the false. The false is sometimes subtly disguised: to detect it is not so easy. It is obvious, for example, that Stalinists—Stalinists of whatever complexion, and along with them, the heirs of Stalin—are summarily to be condemned. I should myself be glad to see them destroyed. But we are not to conclude from this that all the adherents of Trotsky are necessarily to be admitted: there are few of them—

very few—who could make out a case for themselves as candidates for Redemption——"

"How about the Weinburgites, Harry?" the host interrupted with a mischievous look. "Have we got to let them all in?"

"I am raising a serious question," the Marxist, put out, replied. He had passed, without taking account of it, from an attitude of sophisticated scepticism to an acceptance of the crisis as real.

"I'm in fundamental agreement with Harry," the analyst intervened, "except that I'm an orthodox Freudian instead of belonging to a splinter sect."

"Weinburgism is normative Marxism——"

"All right : well, in just the same way, Freudianism for me is normative Freudianism—correct psychoanalytic theory. Sigmund Freud is another of our prophets. You would agree to that, wouldn't you?" He turned to the Messiah.

"In a sense, yes : I grant you——"

"In the deepest sense. And Freud has been as badly betrayed by those who professed to follow him as Marx or Moses has. I should not care to see any of these betrayers redeemed any more than Harry would the Stalinists." His debonair manner was ebbing and allowing to break through its surface the rock of fundamental conviction. "These loose and sloppy impostors, who disregard the discipline of the Freudian method, who cannot see the inevitability of the fundamental Freudian conceptions—who indulge and ruin their patients, who trifle with them and take their money, who leave them in the moral abasement of their unresolved complications, because they cannot face the problems themselves—these problems that require effort, self-mastery, objective thinking—because they cannot face these problems, which involve unpleasant realities and difficult readjustments, any better than the patients can—such quacks should be treated as criminals ! I should be glad to see them all pulverized, beginning with Jung ! And here I agree in principle with what my friend has just said. It is impossible to judge of such matters unless one has been a practising analyst."

"You forget," the Messiah retorted, rising to the challenge to combat, "that I have behind me One who has spoken to Marx and Freud, and who can judge the deviations of their followers better than you can do."

"You forget," said the Marxist, "that every good Jew has that One behind him."

"When we get around to the dead"—the Messiah took higher ground—"Freud and Marx will themselves be judged."

"And the Prophets?" cried the Hebraist. "Are *they* to be judged?"

Though the scholar had for a long time been silent, no one of the company present was more resistant than he. He had been scrutinizing Elijah as the old man ate, and the suspicion of his authenticity had seemed to him conclusively confirmed. There is a Biblical word for *knife*—*m'akhelet*—which is evidently derived from the verb *to eat,* and this has been taken as evidence that the instrument was used at meals. Jealous of the credit of the ancient Jews as pioneers of civilization, the professor was strongly of this opinion, and when he had seen the ninth-century Elijah tearing the chicken apart with his fingers, he had with difficulty repressed his indignation. As the argument grew more heated, this burst. "But this alleged prophet here," he followed up, "it is certainly permitted to judge. I will give you my own judgment. No such Hebrew jargon as his was ever spoken in ninth-century Israel, nor any-where else then or since. This we know with complete certainty!" He turned on Elijah and addressed him in Yiddish : "Haven't I seen you on the stage at the Yiddish theatre?"

Elijah looked up from his plate, then glanced at the Messiah for explanation.

"You mustn't say such things to him," the young man warned the professor. "He's never learned Yiddish—in spite of all the circumcisions he's been to—but he might think you're not being respectful."

The little professor, however, was unable to contain himself. "Tell me"—he renewed the charge, this time speaking in Hebrew pronounced in accordance with his own system—"did you learn that language from the ravens?"

"Look out !" said the Messiah. "Don't do it !"

"Ravens?" The Prophet repeated, lifting his eyebrows in a piercing smile and stretching out both hands towards the viands. "I have no need of ravens here."

"He thinks you're being hospitable," the young man said. "Now, let it go at that. Have the sense to let him alone."

"I simply want to put it on record," said the Hebraist, speaking to the company in English, "that I do not accept their pretentions. I regard them as bare-faced frauds—contemptible blasphemous frauds!"

"Listen!" the Messiah protested. "He still stands high with the Name. Remember what happened to those heathen cultists, when their god let them down on Mount Carmel!"

"Yes : lay off, Lou," intervened the host.

"Well," said the Messiah, rising, "there's no need for us to stay any longer. I'll be seeing you all before long. Any doubts you may still have tonight will, I think, be dispelled tomorrow."

Elijah arose and blessed them. He and the Messiah—in the general silence—left the apartment together, the young man closing the hall door behind them.

"Let's not argue now," said the host. "Let's finish the Seder first."

They took up the Haggadah where they had left it off; went through the thanksgiving hymns punctiliously and rather subduedly. The final words, "To next year in Jerusalem"—familiar though they were—frightened some, put an unexpected question to all. Out of bravado, the Marxist and the analyst—assisted by the vivacious sister-in-law—struck up the children's rhyme, the *Had Gadya,* which parallels *The House that Jack Built,* but this was allowed to peter out.

No one wanted to speak of what had happened. "Well," said the host at last—putting a half-humorous matter-of-fact face on it —"we'll be able to check in the morning whether the Arabs are dropping dead."

But though by this time it was well past midnight, nobody dared to suggest going out to buy a morning paper, and all the guests very soon left.

The Messiah came to himself in his room on East Ninety-Second Street. It was at first an agony of reintegration, of recalling and concentrating in his own single person, the projected multiple selves that had visited the thousands of Seders. Fatigue, incoherence, unbearable strain : gasping from the efforts of self-dispersal, the pangs of organic self-reconstitution, he felt at moments that he could not survive, that he was losing his hold on the world.

Then at last he became aware, in the grey early morning light, of the familiar equipment of his room. He was lying on the wooden bed—close to the floor, with no headboard or footboard—that he had had a local carpenter knock together for him; and opposite, against the wall, stood a desk, bought at second-hand, stuffed and piled with his folders and papers. There were also a small bookcase and some second-hand filing cabinets. On the wall were hung a photograph of Zion and, spread out, the embroidered prayer-shawl he had worn at his confirmation. On a chair beside the bed lay a paper bag, a pasteboard container for coffee and the glazed-paper wrapper of a chopped-egg sandwich, with which he had fortified himself just before taking off for his visits. The foody smell of these was now repellent. On a shelf he caught sight of the alarm clock which he had set for seven the night before, in case he should be still in his trance. He could not make out the time. Had it just gone off without his having heard it? Was it still to go off? He shuddered. How it would crash like a rocket-bomb on his already tortured nerves. Yet he did not reach for his glasses.

At this moment the alarm exploded. He made himself rise to his feet, snatched the clock from the shelf and turned it off. He sat a moment on the side of the bed, then he lay down again. Ignorant of the ravages of dissipation, he had known the abysmal depletions that follow intellectual excess. But the recovery from these had been hastened by the sense of accomplishment, triumph; the tissues of the mind soon mended. This morning there was a lesion that did not heal, a horror of failure, of bafflement lay at the back of his aching brain. He shrank from assembling his experiences, reliving them, extracting their meaning. He tried to curb his natural quickness of mind, to lapse into stupor, to dull his wits. But inertia, self-obfuscation were repugnant to him, impossible for him. Spasmodically, with dim fits of fainting, the powers of his mind revived. More and more swiftly and deftly, like one who sifts the contents of an auction room or sorts out a stacked correspondence, he examined, correlated, analysed his visits of the night before. But below the rapid movements of his mind, the conviction of his mission lay stunned.

Then a deathly collapse engulfed him: "Rejected!" he exclaimed to himself. "Rejected!—I ought to have expected it! They resisted me, repulsed me, mocked me. It's I who am the Suffering Servant of Isaiah, despised and rejected of men !"

But he pulled himself together, sat up, and summoning, affirming the formulas of prayer, he appealed to the Lord aloud.

"I have failed, my Lord," he said. "Your servant is sick in spirit."

Silence : a terrible fear made the young man sit tense on the edge of the bed, hardly daring to breathe.

Then came . the expected Voice, filling, including the room : "You will be made whole again."

"But it hasn't worked out as we thought it would."

Silence : his desperate dread compelled the poor boy to go on, to revert to the self-confident tone with which he had talked to the Deity when he had first unfolded his plans : "Let me give you the picture as I see it. Undoubtedly you can throw more light on it—I beg Thee," he quickly added, lest he seem to qualify Omnipotence, "that Thou wilt aid me to understand Thy will.

"To begin with the Orthodox end : they would give one look at me and throw me out—on account of no earlocks and beard. Well, we more or less anticipated that. I thought—and I believe you approved—that, on the whole, it was more important to make the modernized ones feel at ease, and anyway that was the note we wanted to strike. I was counting on Elijah—though I'd never seen him then—to put it over with the Orthodox, but the trouble is that, being so first-millennial, so rugged, so much the product of a primitive outdoor life, he doesn't look much more like their idea of a Jew than I do. They thought he was crazy and I was a fake. In fact, that's what most of them thought. But the worst of it is that none of them—or almost without exception—is willing to accept my authority. They will accept their rabbi's authority, but —much as they pretend to adore you—they won't recognize the Over-all Power. That's the trouble about a church with no hierarchy. The Catholics could swing it, but we've got no machine. Those fanatical old-timers in Mea Shearim won't accept the Chief Rabbi of Jerusalem. They set their own rabbi up against him, and they couldn't think of imagining a Day of the Lord in which anyone but themselves would come out on top. Of course, they're the lunatic fringe but it's the same with all the Orthodox as against the Reformed. If we got the emigration started, they'd organize resistance against it; they'd work up a counter-propaganda and denounce me as another Sabbatai Zevi. And even those who have no worship are carrying the same narrow spirit into whatever their department is. The Marxists and the analysts and the scholars of every kind all seem to have their element of Mea Shearim. Every field has its own sects, its own rabbis, and the followers of any rabbi can't face the possibility that the disciples of another rabbi may be counted among the righteous. Why, there's even a music expert—a disciple of the Rabbi Schoenberg—who wants to exclude from Redemption all the modern composers who don't practise the pure twelve-tone system. He told me he would refuse absolutely to recognize the competence of our Final Assize unless I could give him the assurance that neither Bloch nor Milhaud would be passed. There's even a literary critic—a rabbi himself, with his own disciples—who says that he can't run the danger of finding himself assigned to a category which might include certain critics who don't subscribe to his doctrine. The core of that doctrine is that— evaluating in moral terms—there are only five novelists in English whose work can be taken seriously.

"And I'm speaking now only of the people that we thought we could more or less count on! You know how the rest of them are. They don't want to go to Israel at all, except maybe for a tourist trip. These city lawyers and doctors and men who have built up businesses—half the time they don't care anything about Judaism. They're making good money somewhere or they're good at their work or both, and beyond that they don't want to be bothered. The only group, so far as I can see, that shows any real interest in the project are the unsuccessful small business and professional men who still go to the synagogue and who hope to better themselves. They think that, when the Day of the Lord comes, their piety may get them further than their abilities ever have. They and a few very young people who go to Hebrew-speaking summer camps and are passionately patriotic about Israel. But nobody else is with us. There's nothing like the response we hoped for."

The Voice replied—the young man listened, in spite of his jaunty tone, with anxious and taut attention. "You must not say 'we,'" the Voice chided. "I was never so hopeful as you. I am no longer quite omniscient, as I used to be. Mankind sometimes gets away from me, as I never allowed it to do in the days of Eden and Babel. I have had my forebodings and doubts."

His confidence in his Deity not fortified, the Messiah fell to blaming his people. "The Jews," he came out with it, "could never agree, and why should we—why should *one* expect them to lay off their disputations even in the shadow of the Judgment Day? But the Exile, the Diaspora have aggravated this weakness. I am sure you are fully aware of the harm that has been done them by Protestantism. Living in Protestant countries, they have taken over the Protestant habits of thought: the idea of deciding for oneself, following one's own conscience, setting oneself up as a judge. Even among those who trust in Thee, blessed be Thy Name, each of them wants to feel that he's got his own private line to you. They're getting to be just like the Protestants—they believe in themselves, not you. Yet they got it out of our Bible—in a way it's there—and if it's there, you—Thou didst put it there. After all, Thou spakest to all kinds of people—Amos the shepherd or anybody could turn out to be a prophet. You must—Thou needs must have known what would eventually happen."

The Voice did not speak for some time. The young man dropped his face and covered his eyes, assuming a reverent attitude but leaving the point he had made.

Then it answered: "Did it ever occur to you that you yourself are lacking in faith, that you have become disrespectful in addressing Me, that you've taken a good deal into your own hands, and that, now that the result does not satisfy you, you are showing a reprehensible impertinence in attempting to take Me to task?"

It was the turn of the Messiah to be silent.

"I am an unworthy servant, Lord!" he cried. "Forgive me for forgetting that, weak though I am, Thy hand will be strong to uphold me. We'll see how they all feel tomorrow when they read about what's happened to the Arabs."

"The Arabs will be spared," said the Voice.

"They'll be spared? But I've promised they would be destroyed. You can hardly go back on that!"

"That would do no good now. If My people do not believe, this sign would not bring them to Zion. They will simply be convinced that the Middle East is a dangerous place to live."

"But if all the Jews are spared?"

"I have some reputation for justice—though I believe you were implying a moment ago that I had not dealt justly with you. The Arabs, at the hands of My people, have already suffered some injustice, and many of My people know it. Why wipe them all out for no end?"

"Wouldn't the world be better without them?"

"They, too, have learned from my Word—they worship Me, too, in their fashion."

The Messiah curbed himself from retorting: "You're getting entirely too broad-minded!"

"But what a garbling it is of Thy Word!" was what he exclaimed aloud.

"You pity your own disappointment," answered God, partly quoting himself, "and shall I not pity Ishmael, that great people of more than twenty million persons, who hardly know their right hand from their left, and also many camels?"

In the irritation caused by dismay, the young man had the impulse to sneer: "Do you have to give me those old gags?" But what he asked was, "There's not to be a Judgment Day?"

"Not at once."

"Am I still the Messiah?"

"You must live like any other man."

"But I've built my whole life up to this—ever since you first called me, ever since I became Bar Mitzvah!" He had to rein himself in again not to cry out: "You can't do this to me! I might have succeeded in the Gentile world. I could have been a big commercial physicist. I was working on the bomb when you took me away—I was one of the coming men. Now I can never go back: after tonight, I'll be listed as a screwball. You wouldn't let me make good with the goys, and now I can't lead my people back to Israel. What do you expect me to do?" But what he said was, "My Lord, be blessed to eternity. Thy servant has failed Thee: forgive him, I beg, and direct him to the path of righteousness. Where shall I turn next?"

"Go back to your old work," said the Voice. "Go on raising money for Israel. Maybe some good will come of it."

VII

Education

*Reflections on the Teaching of Latin**

IN PREPARATION for writing this paper, I asked a Latin professor of my acquaintance—probably one of the most brilliant in the English-speaking world—for a professional explanation of the methods of teaching Latin that were followed in my own school-days and that are still in practice today. He made no attempt to defend them. "It's just like the Court of Chancery at the beginning of *Bleak House*," he said. "Nobody has paid any attention to it or tried to do anything about it for ages." Reassured, I attack the problem. I had feared that my personal experience might have been exceptionally unfortunate—in Greek it was the other way— but I shall assume that it was more or less typical. I apologize for speaking to teachers exclusively in terms of this personal experience. They may well feel that I do not grasp their problems. But I should like to put certain things up to them.

My first drill in Latin—and it was merely drill—was designed to get me into prep school. I remember of it nothing but paradigms, which I endlessly wrote out in the evenings and which seemed to me very much the same kind of thing as algebraic equations; and a difficult progress through Caesar, who impressed me, as he did John Jay Chapman, as "not an author but a stone-crushing machine." It would be possible, no doubt, to make Caesar interesting even to schoolboys in their early teens, but I do not believe it is often done, and in any case the teacher starts in with a discouraging handicap. At prep school, I went on to Cicero, who was

* Originally written for *The Archbishop*, published by Brooks School.

a good deal more complicated and, at my age, hardly more attractive.

The worst feature of these two writers—and also of Virgil, whom I shall come to later—is that neither of them seems to a schoolboy to represent anything imaginable as actual human speech. Caesar appears impersonal to the point of not being human; Cicero, despite his invective, infinitely artificial. It was only in my freshman year at college that, arriving at Plautus and Terence, I was able to see that Latin had once been a spoken language—with colloquial contractions like other languages—in which people transacted business, gossiped, made love and quarrelled. I was exhilarated at finding that a Latin author could be *read* rather than solved like a quadratic equation, and I went through almost the whole of Terence. But I did not find him very distinguished or even enormously amusing; nor, though my professor had a passion for Livy and was excellent on Livy's style, did he infect me in the least with his enthusiasm. In the meantime, I had grown to love Greek, and I continued to take Greek courses through college. I elected a few Latin courses, too, and, exploring the subject for myself, I succeeded in discovering at last the magnificence of Latin poetry. (I may previously have been somewhat prejudiced by having listened to the foolish old *idée reçue* that Greek literature is the real thing and Latin a second-rate imitation.) I also came at last to realize how badly I had been taught.

Now, I find that it is still possible for a student today, as it was forty years ago, to have been through four or five years of Latin and yet, as I have recently had a chance to note, not to have learned, for example, the words for the commonest colours, the most familiar animals, the parts of the body or the seasons of the year. Why?

The answer is : Caesar and Cicero—the military vocabulary of the one, the highfalutin rhetoric of the other. And what is the reason for prescribing these writers? The answer to this is that Caesar, at some remote point of the past, was selected as the only example of classical Latin prose that was simple and straightforward enough for a schoolboy to make his way through, and that Cicero represented the ideal of Latin diction at a time when it was thought essential for every educated man to write Latin.

And why the years of grinding at grammar at the expense of learning to read? This is a part of the ancient tradition of abstract intellectual discipline. The justification for it is the same as the justification for piling problems of algebra on students who have no mathematical interests and who will never have occasion to use algebra. Both at worst have a minimum of practical use. Latin syntax does give us some training in the relation of words in a sentence, as algebra gives us some idea of what is involved in mathematical method; but there is nevertheless a fallacy in this old ideal. It strikes us as rather monstrous when we read of how that intellectual prodigy Karl Marx used to exercise his mental muscles by committing to memory whole pages of languages he did not understand; yet actually our teaching of Latin inflicts something not very different. The student is made to memorize pages of declensions, conjugations and rules for grammatical constructions that mean little or nothing to him as language. Does the minimum of real Latin that the young person acquires in this way serve any useful purpose in later life? The lawyer hardly needs such instruction to pick up the Latin phrases of the law; the student in most scientific fields can learn the terminology of his subject without worrying about Cicero and Caesar. Any modern foreign language that is studied will be more highly inflected than English and will afford such a training in grammatical relations in connection with living speech as can hardly be obtained from Latin. Even the argument that the study of Latin will supply us with a valuable key for understanding the precise meanings of English words originally derived from that language seems to me very dubious. Graduates of our best universities, who have been subjected to years of Latin, not infrequently go on thinking that *jejune* means *callow* and that *transpire* means *occur*.

In my own case, my literary interests impelled me to try to find out what the literature of Rome had to offer; yet I managed to get out of college without really knowing how to read dactylic hexameter in Latin—though I was quite proficient at Homer—and it was only several years later that it dawned on me that all the plays I had been put through in both these languages were written in the same meter and what this meter was—for, in class, we had only been made to translate, never to read in meter. (In a course on Catullus and Horace, we were taught about a few of their commoner meters.) That this ignorance of iambic hexameter (so confusingly called "iambic trimeter") is pretty generally prevalent in this country would seem to be indicated by the failure of writers on Eliot's plays to mention that the meter he uses is an adaptation of this. (He follows the loose Latin version—suggested to him, perhaps, by his study of Seneca—in which the line has come to depend mainly on three stresses; and he has even made a point of varying this, in the traditional Roman way, with passages written in trochaics.) I have known men from the big universities who have been interested enough in classics to elect Greek and Latin courses, yet who turn out to have no idea what is meant by the elegiac meter—which is as if one were to study English literature and never find out what a sonnet is.

But now that Latin, like Greek, has been dropped as a required subject, is there any excuse for continuing to teach it in this slow and perfunctory way? Isn't there now at last a great opportunity to give such students as are able to profit by it some real taste for Latin literature, some real insight into Roman history? Professor David Grene at the University of Chicago tells me that he starts students on Greek at college and soon has them reading Xenophon and Homer. Latin, too, should be started later—though it ought, I think, to be begun in school. It should, of course, be studied only by students who may be expected to devote themselves to teaching, religion or literature, diplomatic or civil service, the more serious kinds of law and politics, or to some branch of science such as archaeology in which it will be certainly needed. Start the student in his Fourth Form year. The objection will at once be made that few boys of fourteen or fifteen have as yet the faintest idea of what sort of careers they want, and that even fewer will care to choose Latin. But there ought, it seems to me, to be two curricula, or two different types of school—one for the boy who will follow, or of whom it is hoped he will follow, the kind of professional career that requires some knowledge of history and something of literary taste, and another for the ordinary person who merely wants to make a living and needs or desires no more than a general education. The better equipped universities at present offer special facilities for young men in the former category.

Should not the better schools do so, too? The choice as to what kind of curriculum—or school—the student was going in for would generally be made by the parents, and once the student was entered for the more exacting curriculum, he would have to achieve some mastery of Latin.

Start him off, then, in his Fourth Form year, and set him to reading and memorizing some story or poem in Latin in the second or third week. The grammar should come with the reading. It is a good deal more efficacious to have the student know a poem by heart—even though he will still for some time be dim about the precise meaning of every word and unable to construe it correctly—than to learn to recite by rote the uses of the subjunctive or the prepositions that take the ablative. This is the way we learn our own language or pick up a foreign language : we get it in its organic form, which is the only form, really, in which it exists. The ideal thing, no doubt, would be to conduct the classes in Latin, but of this perhaps few teachers are capable. I once knew a professor at Yale who decided to adopt this policy with a class in "advanced" Latin. In dismissing the class, he said simply, *"Nunc discedere licet."* Nobody stirred from his seat. It took a week for them all to grasp it. But, failing colloquial Latin, you must make them commit to memory something that will give them the hang of the language. I suggest some Latin version of Aesop. The school-boys of the Middle Ages cut their teeth on the fables, and there was a version in use in New England in the early years of the nineteenth century. The question is which version to use : Phaedrus will hardly do. He is sophisticated, much too difficult. The history of the fables in Latin is long and complicated. They were always being turned from verse into prose, and from prose into verse again. A prose version would be better for our purpose, and the one mentioned above might do ("Select Fables of Aesop, with an English Translation more literal than any yet extant, designed for the readier instruction of Beginners in the Latin tongue, by H. Clarke, Teacher of the Latin Language. The first Walpole Edition from a copy of the latest Edition printed in London. Walpole, New Hampshire, 1802"). By the time the student is done with these, he will at least have learned the names of the animals instead of the vocabulary of military tactics. Now go on to simple poems. I recommend beginning with Catullus' four-line, *"Otium, Catulle, tibi, molestum est."* Besides inculcating a moral which might perhaps appeal to an ambitious boy, this will fix in the memory the vocative form, the words for *city* and *king,* and the fact that the endings in *m* are nasals which must be elided. The same poet's *"Odi et amo"* should leave a sharp little impression and make memorable the verb for *to hate*—the student ought already to know *amo*—and the verb for *not to know.* The next number might be Lesbia's sparrow—a much admired poem, which the teen-ager may find insipid. He will hardly find *"Vivamus, mea Lesbia"* so, and he will learn from it, in a context that brings them out, such important words as *basium* and *semel.* He will also get a weighty gerundive used in a reverberant way. These little poems seem quite spontaneous; Catullus here speaks in a natural voice—almost colloquial republican Latin, before the Augustan grand manner has turned the emotions to marble. You should finish, however, with *"Ave atque vale,"* and explain at the end of the year the components of the elegiac couplet, which is to occupy the class's attention through the whole of the following year.

Up to *"Ave atque vale,"* you can give them the rhythm and simply show them how to mark the stressed syllables. But you must now come to grips with the problems of Latin versification. It is harder to teach than Greek, since the quantities are not always apparent; but it must not be shirked, as it was in most of the courses I took. I propose that the Fifth Form year be devoted entirely to reading as much as possible of Tibullus and Ovid; and I propose that the texts be printed, as the old-fashioned gentlemen's editions were, with circumflexes over the ablative *a* that eliminate one great source of error by distinguishing this long *a* ending from the nominative and accusative ones that are short. The rest will be inevitably a nuisance. In the English public schools up to recently the boys had to learn the quantities by writing elegiacs themselves, and they were flogged if they committed a false one. But this is not practicable here and now; and a good deal can be accomplished by making the student, again, learn some poems by heart, with the quantities right. By the end of his second year of Latin, he ought to be sure of himself in reading both plain hexameters and elegiac couplets. This is much better than starting with Virgil. The style of Tibullus and Ovid is relatively simple and limpid; their vocabulary is more or less standard; and they make few intellectual demands.

The third year—Sixth Form—should, however, be devoted to Virgil, who is the *pièce de résistance* of this poetic banquet. The students should now be well able to handle the normal hexameter, and they can appreciate the variations that Virgil is so skilful at playing on it. Do not start them with the first book of the *Aeneid,* and at no time attempt to persuade them that this epic is a rattling good story. They will soon discover the fraud. The *Aeneid* has none of the movement, none of the ballad quality, of the *Iliad,* and if it is given to students too young, it can seem to them as deadly as Cicero and Caesar. It ought to be approached later, and from a different point of view : as the civilized and self-conscious work it is. The true form and mood of Virgil are those of the eclogues he wrote earlier, and you ought to start off with the first of these. The value of Virgil is immense. Our English descriptive poetry is largely based on a Latin tradition which Virgil exhibits at its best. The representational powers of language seem not fully to have been realized till Rome. The Greeks had been sensitive to sound, but rather vague in their sense of colour, and had no such feeling for substance and bulk, ways of moving and changes of pace, states of weather and natural objects, as is displayed in the poetry of the Romans. You have in Virgil a range of effects unequalled in any other Latin poet.

This is an aspect of literature that I believe to be now much neglected. In the school "rhetorics" used in the United States a hundred years ago, there was a section devoted to it, with examples from Milton and Pope that demonstrated how, for example, "rapid" or "retarded" movement could be represented in verse. Pope and Milton had both learned from the Romans, and when several years ago I gave a little course in this subject—the representational powers of language—at a well-known women's college, I used illustrations from these poets as well as many from Virgil. My impression was that these picked students, even those who had been writing verse, had had little or no conception of what the art of such poets consisted of; but they quickly enough caught on, and we went on to such prose writers as Flaubert and Joyce. Yet they should have been taught all this long before with their Milton and their Virgil. The only one of Virgil's effects which, so far as I now remember, was called to our attention at school was the hackneyed onomatopoeia of *"Quadrupedante putrem sonitu quatit ungula campum."*

Begin, as I have said, with the first Eclogue. If the student can be made to grasp the mechanism as well as the charm of such a passage as the one that is vibrant with the sounds of the bees and the doves (show how Tennyson imitated this passage)—

> hinc tibi quae semper vicino ab limite saepes
> Hyblaeis apibus florem depasta salicti
> saepe levi somnum suadebit inire susurro :
> hinc alta sub rupe canet frondator ad auras;
> nec tamen interea raucae, tua cura, palumbes,
> nec gemere aeria cessabit turtur ab ulmo.

—and the marvellous final line :

> Maioresque cadunt altis de montibus umbrae.

he will have made a good deal of progress in the appreciation of literature. The Fourth Eclogue might also be read, with a discussion of the theories and myths about it. Then go on to the eclogue-like parts of the Georgics : the passage on the Civil Wars at the end of the first section—line 424 to the end—with the picture of the ploughman turning up a skull, followed by that of the nations plunging headlong to war like a runaway chariot; and the episode of Orpheus and Eurydice towards the end of the Fourth Georgic—somewhat difficult like all this Virgil, but one of his masterpieces, which nobody ought to miss.

You should tell them how Virgil came to write the *Georgics,* and what he was trying to do in the *Aeneid,* and you should certainly make them read the Sixth Book of the *Aeneid,* itself a cluster of eclogues (going back, when they come to Palinurus' ghost, to pick up his beautifully Virgilian death at the end of the book before). This will probably be enough (don't worry about Aeneas and Dido—except to explain Dido when she turns up in Hades—which episode is likely to make the boys think that both

Aeneas and Virgil were muffs). They will now have been given a chance to get some sort of all-round idea of Virgil as a great poet rather than having been left bogged in the *Aeneid* with no idea why they have been asked to wade into it.

This will take them through the Sixth Form. In their first year of college Latin, they ought to get more of Catullus, as much as possible of Horace, and some passages at least of Lucretius. Lucretius is, of course, easier to read than Virgil, but it would be wise to put him off till college, when the student is more mature and can grapple with the poet's philosophy. The remaining three years of college should be occupied entirely with prose : the historians (Caesar, Livy, Tacitus) and Cicero. The student ought now to be old enough to take an historical interest in Caesar, and he will be able to cope with Cicero. He should have Roman politics explained to him, and the development in the ancient world of the writing of human history, and he should be given collateral reading, ending with chunks of Gibbon. If the student is sufficiently interested, he should be given a chance, in elective courses, to pick up the authors skipped, and to go on to the dessert, nuts, liqueurs and after-dinner conversation of the writers of the "Silver Age"; Seneca, Juvenal, Martial, Petronius and the rest. But the programme I have outlined above is enough for literacy in Latin.

These, of course, would be special students; but I do not think this programme impractical. The old method should, in any case, be scrapped. The effect of it is to consume a good deal of time and yet to leave the student quite unable to penetrate the Latin language. To quote again the distinguished professor whom I mentioned at the beginning of this paper : it is as if years of study of the violin were to get the pupil no further than the first two positions of the left hand.

The Need for Judaic Studies

Another feature of my ideal university would be courses in the literature and history of the Jews for students—both Gentile and Jewish—who should never have had any Hebrew but who should want to inform themselves on these subjects. Matthew Arnold has said that our civilization has been based on the heritage of three great cultures: the Hebrew, the Greek and the Roman. He had been reading Spinoza and Heine, and his general view of history had been influenced profoundly by Renan. But he would never have made such a formulation on the basis of what they had taught him in English schools. One is offered certain opportunities for finding out about Greece and Rome; but the approach to the Hebrew record was, in Arnold's time, and more or less is still, diverted by religious bias. The supposed divinity of Jesus has caused a wrinkle in history not unlike Einstein's fold in space, which used to be compared to a hill that looks like flat earth from above: one cannot see that the hill is there except by observing the fact that everybody goes around it. You may, of course, have Old Testament courses that are compulsory on the prep school level; but these come under the head of religious instruction, and they lead on to a study of the New Testament which has to be conducted in such a way that no parent can possibly be shocked. And what about the universities? In my time at Princeton—1912–16—a course in the Old Testament was offered by a competent Biblical scholar, the late Dr. Lucius Miller. I took the second half of this course and I learned from it quite a lot; but in the meantime Dr. Miller had published a book—not in the least subversive for anyone but a strict fundamentalist—in which an attempt was made to deal with Jesus as an historical figure, and this so alarmed the Presbyterians who lurked always in the background at Princeton that they brought pressure to bear on the

Board of Trustees, where the Presbyterian influence predominated, and Dr. Miller was immediately dropped. On the Orthodox Jewish side, the resistance to objective historical study is apparently just as strong. On a recent visit to Israel, I learned with surprise from a scholar at the Hebrew University that he was giving what he told me was, so far as he knew, the first non-religious course in ancient Jewish history that had ever been offered in any seat of learning. He disregarded the Bible as Scripture and co-ordinated its historical evidence with the evidence of other texts and the findings of archaeology.

What is needed for the secular student are courses that would correspond to those that are now offered in the histories of Greece and Rome and in Greek and Latin literature in translation—courses that would enable him to correlate the adventures and achievements of the Jews with those of the rest of the world. I should propose a, say, two-year course with something like the following programme. My reading in this field is limited and probably somewhat capricious, and my suggestions may well seem ill-chosen to persons who know it well. I want merely to indicate the kind of thing that I think it would be useful for people to know, and the spirit—as unbiased as possible—in which it ought to be approached.

First Year : The Old Testament taught by the method described above, with sidelights on the Hittites, the Ugarites and the other lost episodes of history that have recently been brought to light. This course should include some apocrypha as well as a few selections from the intertestamental literature, such as *The Testaments of the Twelve Patriarchs,* with its novel-like developments of the Bible stories and its unmistakable parallels with the Gospels. What ought to be done at this point about the literature of the Dead Sea sect, in whose library manuscripts of the Testament of Levi and of others of the pseudepigraphal writings have been found in the original Hebrew? I assume that in this ideal university there would also be offered courses in the history and literature of Christianity, and the documents from the Dead Sea library should probably be studied at the beginning of these. In any case, the wrinkle in history of which I have spoken above should be firmly ironed out, and the development of Christianity be traced from Judea rather than Heaven. The first year of the Jewish course should go on to selections from Josephus : his autobiography and parts of his histories. The recurrence should be pointed out, in Jewish careers and characters, of their Biblical prototypes. Josephus has something of Jacob and something of his namesake Joseph. Like Jacob, he becomes an adventurer, resourceful and sometimes unscrupulous, yet—as Jacob from time to time is aroused by the call of God—aware of his obligation, the obligation to God of the Jew, to rise above human injustice; but Josephus' relation to the Romans has something of Joseph in Egypt, in his rôle of right-hand man of Pharaoh : Josephus ends living in Rome, a protégé of the Roman emperor. This first year might come to a close with some account of the rebellion of Bar-Kochba, the last effort by the Jews in the ancient world—defeated in 135 A.D.—to establish their political independence.

Second Year : Begin with the Talmud. There is a small book, now out of print, which contains two admirable essays on the subject, elucidations for Gentile readers, by Arsène Darmesteter and Emanuel Deutsch. The class might begin with these, which will give them the historical background, and then go on to extracts from the text itself in the recent Soncino translation, which is said to be a good deal better than the earlier one by Michael L. Rodkinson. The Kabbala should, of course, get attention, but, having given it none myself, I can make no suggestions about it. The class need not be made to take much of the hair-splitting of Jewish observances, but they ought to know enough about them to understand why Orthodox Jews behave in the way they do. The whole history of the Jewish code—through Maimonides and Joseph Caro—should probably at this point be outlined. The great thing here, it seems to me, to understand is the principle by which the Law was adapted to changing conditions by new ways of inter-preting the scriptural text. These methods of interpretation—*pilpul* and all the rest—will otherwise seem gratuitously far-fetched, fantastic. Now the Karaite movement should be studied, the eighth century revolt from the Talmud. The strange story of the discovery by Solomon Schechter, in 1896, in the Genizah of a Cairo syna-gogue, of a collection of Karaite manuscripts, and their tie-up with

the Dead Sea documents, should be brought to the class's attention. They should know something of the classic formulations of
the position of the Jew through the centuries: Philo, Saadia,
Jehuda Halevi, Maimonides, etc. This might well begin with a
reading of that very curious document, the Epistle of Aristeas, a
legendary account of the making of the Greek translation of the
Bible known as the Septuagint. The author is apparently a Jew
pretending to be a courtier of Ptolemy Philadelphos in the third
century of the Christian era, and he tells his supposed correspondent that Ptolemy's great desire to acquaint himself with the
Hebrew Scriptures has led him to bring in from Jerusalem seventy-
two Jewish scribes, six elders from each tribe, for the purpose of
having the book translated. He entertains them with splendid
banquets every evening for seven days and puts to each one in turn
a philosophical question, with the reply to which he is invariably
delighted. The visitors also explain to him the reasons for their
Jewish observances. When these ceremonies are over, the seventy-
two scribes are set to translate the Bible, and they accomplish this
in exactly seventy-two days. The teacher should lecture also—
though the class should not have to wade through it—on Justin
Martyr's dialogue with the Rabbi Trypho. Though the dialogue is
written by Justin himself and though Justin does almost all the
talking, this early Christian polemic has the effect of making the
modern reader sympathize profoundly with Trypho and the Jewish
point of view. Christianity in the second century is still a new
movement which is forced to fight, to impose itself by fair means
or foul, and the early Christian apologist sounds like nothing so
much as a Communist talking down a recalcitrant opponent.
Surrounded by a group of listeners, Justin tells Trypho not to
waste his time with unnecessary disputation, since he is just about
to take the boat, puts arguments into the rabbi's mouth to which
he has the answers ready, and demonstrates in an harangue which
must have taken hours, that the Bible, from beginning to end, is
a prophecy of the coming of Jesus the Christ. At the close of this,
Trypho thanks Justin and wishes him a safe voyage—a gesture of
which Renan says truly that, if Justin's account is correct, it is
one of the most courteous actions of which a record has reached
us. In the rabbinical literature itself, there is much that is quaint

and amusing as well as so much that is noble, and the class should get plenty of stories along with the Judaic doctrine—Jewish folklore, from Tobit and the Talmud to the later Dybbuk and Golem. They should read, in connection with the Hassidic movement, Ansky's play on the former theme—like *Wozzeck* and *The Playboy of the Western World,* a unique and enduring work that does not fit into any category. For history—beginning with the Diaspora— I recommend Cecil Roth's *A Short History of the Jewish People.* This compact and well-written book is such a sure-fingered summary as can only be made on the basis of a lifelong experience of one's subject, and it would have the special value, in connection with such a course as I am outlining, of offsetting any tendency to present the various phases of Jewish life exclusively in terms of religion, since Roth is especially full on the worldly activities of the Jews—in politics, in commerce, in finance. I suggest that the course break off with the figure of Moses Mendelssohn, and the emergence of the Jew in the West from his segregated and inbred condition to full citizenship of the modern world.

In the second year of my programme, a special difficulty will have to be faced. When the Anglo-Jewish historian Sir Lewis Namier was asked why he did not write the history of the Jews instead of that of the British Parliament, he is said to have replied that the Jews had no history, "only a martyrology"; and it is true that, once Bar-Kochba is dead, any attempt to write Jewish history is likely to become depressing. But the tracing of the streams of the Diaspora, the tenacity and continuity of Jewish life have their own kind of fascination. In any case, the main facts of Jewish survival, the main features of Jewish thought, ought to be common knowledge. On the Gentile side, to make them so would be a safeguard against anti-Semitism. As has been said by a Jewish writer, the Jew is much better informed about the Gentiles among whom he lives than the Gentiles are about him. The average non-Jewish American—and I suppose it is more or less true elsewhere—takes his Jewish compatriots for granted as neighbours, as business associates, as artistic or professional colleagues. And yet there is a mystery behind them which does not exist in other backgrounds. We have seen that the average man may suddenly become persuaded that these people he has been taking for granted are all part of an insidious conspiracy to undermine the world as he knows it. It has lately, to be sure—what with Schocken books, the profusion of the Jewish press and the constant publicity of Israel—become easier to inform oneself. But the Jews should have at least as much place in our picture of civilization as they have had in our heritage of superstition. And not merely the Gentile would profit from this. To make a complete break, as so many of the Jews have done, with a traditional religious authority— especially in the case of a religion that puts one at a disadvantage with the society in which one lives—is likely to cause a rejection of everything connected with it. You have children of Orthodox parents who seek to become "assimilated," and children whose parents, and even whose grandparents, were already assimilated, who have never read a Jewish book or a book about the Jews, who do not care to hear about anything Jewish. But to cut oneself off from one's forebears is likely to produce bad effects : it sets up strains and repressions; the habits of mind persist though the history that formed them is hidden. My programme would "fill" such people "in" : it would give them the knowledge they need.

These courses should be taught by a Jew. Few non-Jews would be competent to teach it, and these are likely to be top scholars, occupied with special research. Jewish subjects, I have noticed, besides, have a way of becoming denatured when they pass through non-Jewish hands. Let the student be exposed to a Jewish scholar, expounding, without inhibition, the traditions and the point of view of his own so important people.

The Problem of English

And what about the teaching of English? What, exactly, does it mean to "teach English" in the United States?

Again I revert to my own experience. As a child, I imagined that a permanent antagonism existed between my father and me, that I was always, in tastes and opinions, on the opposite side from him. This was due, I can see, looking back, to a certain intellectual intolerance on my side as well as on his. But he was not an easy man to talk to : he almost eliminated give-and-take, for his conversation mostly consisted of either asking people questions in order to elicit information or telling them what to think. Our dinners at home, when we had no guests and there were only my parents and I, were likely to turn into lectures. My mother at her end of the table was—prematurely—so very deaf that she could not have any real interchange with my father at the other end, and my conversation with him usually took the form either of his asking my view of some question, then immediately squelching this view and setting me right on the subject, or of explaining at length, but with an expert lucidity, some basic point of law or government. So much did I take for granted our polarization that I was startled to realize one day that I was imitating my father's signature—my name was the same as his—which, like his writing in general, was completely illegible but quite beautiful in a graphic way, as if he had invented a calligraphy in order to conceal his meaning from everyone except himself. This handwriting had thus also its arrogance as well as its curious elegance, and I found myself emulating these.

But it was not until after my father's death—in 1923—that I had a new revelation of the extent of my mimicry of him. In going through his speeches, briefs and other papers, I became for the first time aware how well he had expressed himself. His style had,

I saw, a purity quite exceptional in a public—or quasi-public— figure in New Jersey in the early nineteen hundreds, and his language was always distinguished by a silvery quality of clearness —I remember how he used to make fun of the pompous laboured prose of Cleveland—which led me to understand his enthusiasm for the style of Stevenson, which I myself rather disliked. I realized now—and again with surprise—that I had been imitating this literary style as well as his penmanship. For my methods in writing had seemed to me personal : though I had imitated Shaw, Henry James and a number of other writers, I had consciously corrected these tendencies and was unconscious of my principal model. Since I had rarely heard my father in court or listened to his public speeches, I must have picked up his style mainly from his dinner-table lectures.

Some years after my father's death, I began making notes of his vocabulary and his characteristic phrases, and for the first time I took account of how old-fashioned his English was. He would say, for example, "It rains" or "It snows"—as the characters in Jane Austen do—instead of "It is raining," "It is snowing"; "It makes no matter" for "It doesn't matter." He would some-times correct himself if he fell into the current usage of "*a* hotel" and make it "*an* hotel." He was the only living person I have ever known who used the exclamation "Zounds !" He was in-capable of any other profanity, never even said "Good God !" or "Damn !" and his "Zounds" had a nuance of humour, but he did not regard it as a period piece. He was especially fond of such metaphors as "weltering around in a Dead Sea of mediocrity"— something I was warned not to do, when my school marks were not up to scratch—it was the worst fate with which he could threaten me. He was very much annoyed one day when, on our way home from one of his speeches, I undertook to inform him that the word he had wanted to use was *cataclysm,* not *cataclasm. Cataclasm* was then so archaic that I did not even know it existed and that it differed in meaning from *cataclysm.* I decided, in any case, at the moment of discovering in the writing of his papers the model for my literary style that this model was a valuable heritage, like the table pieces of silver of the Paul Revere silversmith period which had come to me from his side of the family.

Later on, at my prep school—Hill—I had been trained in traditional English by an extremely able English teacher—Dr. John A. Lester—who was himself an Englishman. He drilled us in sentence structure, grammar, the devices of "rhetoric" and prosody, as if we had been studying a foreign language; and we were made to take very seriously—as I have never, indeed, ceased to do—the great Trinity : Lucidity, Force and Ease. I have valued this training so much that I have always contended that English ought to be taught in this country by Englishmen. But this brings us to the crux of the problem : should Americans attempt to learn British English : and, if so, to what extent? There have been moments when I have seriously wondered whether my pieces of pre-revolutionary silver were adequate for modern use. I have sometimes become so bored with the language in which I wrote articles—the monotony of the vocabulary and the recurrence of routine formulas—that I would find it a great relief to get away from this kind of writing and give myself a freer hand in a play or a piece of fiction in which I could make people talk as contemporary Americans did. I also tried injecting some current slang into my purely critical writing, but I found that this was likely to jar and that I later had to take it out. With my own education based mainly on the literature and language of England, I sometimes envied H. L. Mencken, with his half-German education, which seemed to make it easier for him to play on "the American language." I was then and still am all in favour of the free development and the literary use of a semi-independent American language, but I cannot face without a shrinking the state of things predicted by Mencken, in which illiterate usage would eventually prevail in the United States—so that our grammar would be reduced to, for example, such conjugations—or non-conjugations —as *I was, you was, he was; we was, you was, they was.* It is not so much, however, that our few surviving inflections are important as that the logic of syntax should not be lost. With all the considerable divergence between British and American idiom, the structure of the language is still the same—or ought to be the same, for otherwise we should have no structure : we should get nothing but woolly writing, incapable of expressing anything either elegantly or exactly.

I am aware of the special problems that exist in American public schools—that in localities where most of the pupils are the children of foreign parents, themselves illiterate in their native tongues, the instructor must sometimes be satisfied to teach them any English at all, that to exact from them a standard of correctitude becomes quite out of the question. I know that in some of our schools it is even as much as the teacher can do to avoid being murdered by his more aggressive students. But there ought to be institutions in which the abler kind of student could be taught to handle language competently. In my ideal university, I should have, as a general requirement, most rigorous courses in English, and I should have them all taught by Englishmen. Every student in every department would have to pass examinations in the accurate writing of English. Those specializing in scientific fields as well as the philosophers and historians would have their papers graded—except, of course, the kind that consist of equations—by the teachers in the English department as well as by their other professors, and, although it might be sometimes unfair to make it an invincible rule that no incompetent writer should ever be allowed to graduate, the gradings for precise expression should be given a good deal of importance.

The use of the English language as an instrument for analysis and exposition is one inheritance from England that we cannot afford to scrap. In the sciences, this logical and concrete style—as I have heard a Russian scientist say—possesses certain decided advantages over either German or French, which both, in their respective ways, so much tend to run to abstractions. In English it is easier to follow the argument, to see what the data are and to know what conclusions have been drawn from them in terms of a practical process. It is handier to describe a species, a country, a disease, a geological formation; to lay down the rules for a game, to give directions for navigation. In America, we have done a good deal to make a mess of this excellent medium. In my youthful days as an editor, I had once to prepare for publication a series of articles by the late John Dewey on a trip he had made to China. This ought really not to have involved him in obscurity, since he was merely telling what he had seen and the opinions to which it had led him; but when I came to edit the articles, I found that they both called for and resisted revision in a peculiarly exasperating way. It was not only a question here of clarifying the author's statements but of finding out what he meant; and when you did get the sense of his meaning, there was no way of straightening out the language : you would have had to try to give his meaning in a language of a different kind. But John Dewey, as I presently found out—though typical—was not by any means the worst American writer on education. Later on, the liberal weekly for which I worked ran a supplement on this subject, and the articles we received were incredible. How, I wondered, could a man set up as an authority on teaching the young when he was not himself sufficiently well-educated to have mastered the rudiments of writing. As for my experience with articles by experts in anthropology and sociology, it has led me to conclude that the requirement, in my ideal university, of having the papers in every department passed by a professor of English might result in revolutionizing these subjects—if indeed the second of them survived at all.

But even in the "Humanities" department there is a serious crisis in literacy. How can you write about a literary subject—especially some great artisan of speech—when you yourself are hardly articulate, can scarcely express the most commonplace thoughts? At most, you can unearth a few unknown facts, point out some unsuspected sources. If you even, with no knowledge of the literary art, do not attempt anything more interesting than the dreary *"exposition des textes"* that has become a kind of standard academic product, you are likely to misread a language which you have never properly learned. Among the products of American teachers of such feeble qualifications, I have encountered some appalling cases. Some years ago—in 1939—I taught at the summer school of one of the biggest—and, I believe, one of the best—of the Western universities. A man who had been giving a course in contemporary English literature had gone abroad for the summer, and I was asked to grade the papers of his students, who had taken their examination after he left. Among the authors studied were Virginia Woolf, Yeats and Joyce—one of the greatest of English poets and two of the greatest masters of the harmonics of English prose; but the papers of the students dismayed me as a hideous revelation of the abysses of non-education that are possible in the United States. Hardly one of them could write and punctuate a respectable English sentence. One paper—like Molly Bloom's soliloquy—had been poured out with no punctuation except for an occasional full stop. In response to the question : "Explain the symbolism of Yeats's *The Winding Stair*," another of the examinees had written the following answer : "As Yeats goes up the winding stair he has a kind of feeling like his old aristocratic past is coming back on him again." This was clearly not the fault of the teacher, a highly competent Britisher, well known as a writer on the subjects he was teaching. The failure had occurred further back. The truth was, of course, that such students should never have been allowed to take such a course at all. They ought to have been learning the use of the comma and the difference between a conjunction and a preposition; they ought to have been standing at blackboards diagramming compound sentences. Another incredible example : a young man, the friend of a friend, once brought me for my criticism a manuscript of his poems. So many kinds of liberties are countenanced—in the way of off-rhymes and irregular rhythms—in the writing of modern poetry that I did not at first question these verses from the technical point of view, but I gradually became suspicious, and when I called the attention of the author to bad metrics and impossible rhymes, I discovered not only that he knew nothing of metrics, had never been told that such a thing existed, but that he did not even understand rhyme, not having grasped the principle that it is the syllables with the accent that have to match, that you cannot rhyme *picture* with *pure*. Yet he had been graduated from an Eastern university which, if not very strong in the Humanities, is of excellent reputation and supposed to keep up a decent standard. He had specialized in American literature and had also had a course in Shakespeare, but it had never been explained to him at any point what kind of verse Shakespeare had written; he seemed, in fact, to have read it as prose. As for his own productions, he had simply seen modern poems in the current "avant-garde" magazines, and had tried to turn out something of the kind himself. (This experience has left me with terrible doubts about some of the stuff that is printed as verse in these literary magazines.) I ought to mention that this touching young man had also been going to classes intended for instruction in the writing of verse at the YMHA in New York, where his writings had been subjected to the scrutiny of a not-unknown poet. But, even after this, it remained for me to break it to him that poetry was an art with rules. It was not that he was stupid : on the contrary, I gave him an hour's instruction and found that he could soon identify the various metrical feet of which till that moment he had never heard. Still another student —from the largest university in the East—told me that he "wanted to write" and turned out to be equally ignorant of the medium that Shakespeare used. He was under the impression that blank verse was any verse that did not rhyme. He had taken one of those courses of miscellaneous classics in translation that are a feature of the modern curriculum, and had been through *The Divine Comedy* without being able to say whether it was written in prose or verse. He did not seem even to know whether the English translation was prose or verse. I was not able to tell him, because he did not know the name of the translator.

VIII

Science

*In the Galapagos**

THE ZOOLOGIST. I see you are not afraid of me.

THE IGUANA. Why should I be? I have encountered sea lions before, and they have never done me any harm.

THE ZOOLOGIST. The tropic-birds that come to breed on the crater-slopes of Daphne are conditioned in a different way from you other inhabitants of the islands. They snap at me with their jagged beaks when I try to go near their nests. They know that I am not a sea lion: they recognize me as a man, and they have had some experience of men on the mainland.

THE IGUANA. We iguanas are afraid of nothing; we know we are the masters of life. The inferior family of lizards have their causes for alarm, I believe: they are so small that the hawks can catch them and they live in continual danger. But we iguanas know very well there is nothing in the universe that can harm us. Lie down beside us here on the rock and enjoy a good stupefying doze.

THE ZOOLOGIST. I would rather converse with you a little. I have come a long way to see you. I have made it my business to travel among the animals and to find out all I can about them, because I believe that they hold the key to mysteries I am trying to solve. And since no other creatures like you, no other marine

* The scientific summaries of this dialogue—suggested by reading Mr. William Beebe's book *Galapagos* and first published in 1925—are to some extent out of date, and the tone is a good deal more exuberant than it is possible to be at sixty, but I still see these problems in the same terms.

iguanas, are, so far as we know, to be found in the world, I have naturally made a point of coming here.

THE IGUANA. I cannot help you to clear up any mysteries. So far as we lizards are concerned, everything in life is a mystery.

THE ZOOLOGIST. You talk as my own race once talked, but as we do not talk any longer. When my ancestors interrogated animals, their questions were purely rhetorical : they did not expect any answers.

> Tiger ! Tiger ! burning bright
> In the forests of the night . . .
>
> In what distant deeps or skies
> Burnt the fire of thine eyes ? . . .
>
> What the hammer, what the chain,
> Knit thy strength and forged thy brain?

The man who addressed the tiger in this fashion was completely resigned to the mystery; he became exalted in contemplating it. But I can no longer be satisfied by the contemplation of something which I do not understand, and it is only in the clearing-up of mysteries that I taste my exaltation. I have come to put to you a similar question, but I mean to make you answer it.

THE IGUANA. Your trouble is wasted; I have nothing to say. I can only recommend a warm siesta—the most satisfying thing in the world.

THE ZOOLOGIST. And yet when the first of our investigators, our scientists, came among you, nearly a hundred years ago, you islanders put a clue in his hand. Hitherto, as I say, we had been resigned to accepting all life as a mystery—to supposing that each kind of animal was the product of a separate creation. But when Charles Darwin came to these islands and observed that each one had its special species—its tortoises, its finches, its plants—each of them quite distinct from the species on the other islands and from similar creatures on the mainland, and yet fundamentally alike, with an obvious family likeness which outweighed their variations, it occurred to him that they might all have derived from some remote common ancestor and that the differences he noticed among them might be merely the result of the various conditions which prevailed in the various islands. Were they not, then, all branches of the same set of families which, through some accident, had been isolated from one another for a number of generations? It was as if the Galapagos had been specially arranged as an elegant demonstration of the process by which species change.

THE IGUANA. We iguanas have always been the same, and there is only one family of us. We are immutable.

THE ZOOLOGIST. You are mistaken. If you were to travel inland here you would find a quite different species, unlike you in habits, shape and colour. Where you have webbed feet and flattened tails, because you have to get about in the sea; where you have strongly developed claws, because you have to climb the rough rock, *they* have only such claws and such tails as they require for the easy savannas; and where your skins are black like your lava-beach, theirs are yellow like their cactus flowers. Yet both of you are the offspring of a common stock, and the differences which have arisen between you are the differences between sea and land.

THE IGUANA. I have not noticed our colour deepening or our claws growing any longer. I can assure you that every generation of us is exactly like the one before.

THE ZOOLOGIST. But in the past they have certainly changed; and they may still be changing today. You will not deny that, as individuals, you differ somewhat among yourselves. Well, the scientist of whom I spoke saw that the iguanas with the flattest tails and the feet which tended most to be webbed would be in the most advantageous situation for supporting life on the shore, because they would more easily be able to swim, and therefore better able to get seaweed to eat. They would survive the others and interbreed and perpetuate their characteristics, which with time would become intensified and the common characteristics of the race. So, not only did it appear that two kinds of iguanas might be bred from a common ancestor, but even that, at some earlier period, the iguanas and the smaller lizards might have had a common parent, too. And, why not, if this were true, all the lizards and all the tortoises and snakes, which all have three-chambered hearts and all are covered with scales? Why not, on the other hand, the whole race of reptiles, and on the other, the whole race of birds—since their feathers, in their earliest stages, are almost the same as your scales? We have found the skeleton of a very ancient animal, half reptile and half bird. May it not be your common grandfather? And, in that case, may it not be that all of us animals who have backbones and nervous systems that stem from them—iguana, bird, sea lion and man—are related to one another? And, for that matter, why not all creatures which have bodies that are basically tubelike : we vertebrates have these in common with the most rudimentary jellyfish or worm? Why not all the creatures that are born from cells and that build themselves up from cells? Why not in short, all living beings?—the seaweed that makes your diet as well as you that use it for the building of cells, and I as well as you?

THE IGUANA. We iguanas have nothing in common with the lesser families of lizards. You are talking mischievous nonsense. They run true to their nature and we to ours. If our tails, among ourselves, individually vary in shape, if our claws are not all the same length, the differences are very slight. It is not possible that differences so vast as those between ourselves and the other lizards could have arisen from variations so tiny.

THE ZOOLOGIST. But this process has been going on through a period of millions of years. Incalculable generations of the gradual development of life must have gone to produce an iguana. And I should also explain that it is possible for very wide variations to suddenly appear without warning. Some scientists believe that it is these and not the lesser variations which have brought the species to their present forms. For all I know, your flattened tails may have come into being, as it were, overnight, when a brood of iguanas that had them was one day unexpectedly hatched.

THE IGUANA. Then there *was* a special creation?

THE ZOOLOGIST. Not at all. The sudden variations are accidents like the others. For one that advances the species, there are many in wrong directions. And they are actually not so sudden as they look. The young iguana was once an egg, and the egg was once a tiny cell, which multiplied by dividing and grew gradually into an iguana. Now, as each of the parts of the body is developed from its own particular cells, a cell lost or a cell superadded might produce a different sort of creature.

THE IGUANA. But how do these cells you speak of become superadded or lost?

THE ZOOLOGIST. That is something we have not yet found out.

THE IGUANA. Then you are only putting back the creation to an earlier stage of development?

THE ZOOLOGIST. I should also explain that the physical conditions under which the animal lives must influence what he is. You yourself, for example, are something more than the residuum of a sifting-out of the iguanas best adapted to the Galapagos coast : you are also a product of the moulding of the tides in which you swim, of the equatorial sun which warms you, of the seaweed on which you live. Whether, however, you inherit the effects of these things or merely a susceptibility to being affected by them, we have not yet been able to determine.

THE IGUANA. But that is absurd. You can see for yourself that these boulders around us here have been played on by the same sea and sunlight and surrounded by the same seaweed as I have; yet they have not become iguanas. You talk as if I were merely an adding-up of these things you call influences and accidents; yet I know I am an entity, a separate force, something complete in myself. I can assure you that, if I have been made at all, it is not the sun and sea that have made me, but I that have made myself.

THE ZOOLOGIST. Yet these boulders and yourselves, as you must admit, have certain characteristics in common : you, like them, are greyish-black, and their backs are dull and rough like yours. From a little way off, in fact, it is impossible to tell you apart.

THE IGUANA. But we are able to swim and crawl about, and have the power of begetting more iguanas, while the boulders can do nothing at all. And we swim because we will to swim; crawl because we will to crawl; and lay eggs because we will to perpetuate a unique and superior race.

THE ZOOLOGIST. Very well; but such simple assertions mean nothing at all to us scientists. Even assuming that, by willing to swim, you eventually acquire the knack and develop flat tails and webbed paws, it is the business of us scientists to study that will, to find out whence it first arises, what constitutes it and how it works.

THE IGUANA. My dear fellow, you are wasting your time. You will never master life by that method. As one animal to another, I can only advise you to follow your natural instinct without worrying about what makes it work. That is the great force that drives us—instinct! Let it carry you from triumph to triumph! Let it guide you to the passionate enjoyment of the fullness of animal life. Just at present my instinct directs me to relax from this conversation, to drop my head and take a brief nap. I am sure that you must feel the same yearning. *(The Iguana closes his eyes.)*

THE ZOOLOGIST. "As one animal to another"—so you animals are always saying to me! On my way here, one night in Panama, I went out to hunt in the jungle. I was equipped with a jack-light on my forehead, and everywhere I looked I saw animals gazing out at me with burning eyes. That was all I could see—their eyes, which reflected the light from the lantern—so that I shot a large toad and a crayfish, thinking they were crocodiles, and almost fired at a spider mistaking it for a possum. Arachnid, crustacean, amphibian, mammal—as we think ourselves so clever in calling them—they all seemed much the same in the dark, and if they had had jack-lights like me, they could hardly have told me from one of themselves. Here we are, I thought, all staring at one another with similar pairs of eyes, each afraid for his life—all animals alert in a jungle! Yet I could see what they could not see, for I could see with the eyes of the mind—I could see both beyond and below them. I looked out upon a different universe from theirs of the jungle dark or from yours of the island shore.

THE IGUANA *(without opening his eyes).* My own is quite good enough : there is everything necessary in it.

THE ZOOLOGIST. None the less, while your eyes are concealing your world, let me tell you for a moment of mine. When you open your eyes and look out, you will behold only the barren coast and the level and quiet sea; when I approach you, you think only of a sea lion—another animal entity, another will, like yourself. But when I look out, I see something different : a vast interaction of factors, functioning with infinite complexity. For me ocean, coast and iguana are both clusters of smaller units and constituents of larger ones. This solid scene first dissolves into numberless billions of entities, each ten million times as small through as the width of my little finger nail. These entities are electric charges; and I distinguish two different kinds, which mutually attract one another.

I see that the charges of one of these types are revolving around those of the other at an inconceivable rate of speed; in some cases, a single particle revolving around another particle, and, in others, a swarm of nearly a hundred whirling about in as many as six successive rings, with a group made up of both kinds of particles, and itself in revolution, at the centre. When one of these electrons, as we call them, shifts from one ring to another, it accomplishes this instantaneously, and, if it shifts from a larger to a smaller ring, it loses a quantity of energy, which you see given off as light. The charge of the revolving electrons always equals the charge of the central group; but when the outer ring becomes overcrowded by the number that is necessary to strike this balance, it allows the outer ring of another system, which has room for extra electrons, to take over a few of these; and the two interlocked groups—called atoms—adjust themselves to one another and travel about together. The same kind of thing happens when the centre of one of these systems has too few or too many electrons. I can see that, as a matter of fact, all the atoms have combined in this way and that they have done so according to definite laws. Some atoms have a double capacity for attraction and are able to attract two atoms of the kind with the least capacity; others only balance with three, and so on up to six. And even beyond this there are certain kinds which, by internal attractions among groups, are able to combine in associations running into thousands. I see all the air about us as composed of certain of these atom-groups—called molecules, "little masses"—moving in straight lines very rapidly in every direction and continually colliding with one another; I see the ocean as a thicker mass, a mixture of the groups which appear in the air with certain other groups, but moving about much less rapidly than the molecules in the air and beginning to stick together. The molecules themselves, in fact, tend to combine—as many as sixty to one—to form larger aggregations. And I see the rocks and the lava-beach built up of these larger units, fixed in regular formations called crystals. Whether the molecules combine in a gas, like the air, in a liquid, like the water, or in a solid, like the rock, depends on whether they have been subjected to a higher or a lower temperature; and I have a quite accurate grasp of the laws which govern these changes. I see our animal bodies composed also of aggregations but in a more unstable condition than those that make up the rock; they are continually breaking down and reforming between, on the one hand, a state of fluid and, on the other, a state of jelly, in which last condition the molecules have linked themselves together in a network that looks like foam. In a single human body, there are thirty million such units, all organized in a great community—all reacting with one another and with the gases and solids about them—some alive and performing their rhythms of dissolution and agglutination, others dead and pressed into service as scaffoldings and walls to form envelopes for the live ones. These units we call cells; they average in length a five-hundredth of the width of my little finger nail; I see them filled with a greyish jelly which is sprinkled with little grains and strung through with a net of threads that stretch from the sides to a body in the centre. Near this is a larger nucleus containing its own network, body and grains. But in such an organic community, there are different kinds of cells designed to play different rôles. All of them have breathing grains for the purpose of splitting up a particular kind of molecule, to which we have given the name oxygen, and supplying the cell with its separate atoms; but other grains perform different duties, according to the function of the cell. Some store up fat, for nourishment; others starch, for fuel in the muscles; some contain the material for nerves; others the material for eggs; still others the colours of the skin, and so forth. One finds also, cells of a similar kind more closely banded together and collaborating in their office. These are tissues; some breathe, some breed, some give you the power of movement. They are working together in your body in a way that I understand, but which I haven't time now to rehearse. The point is that the whole community is exchanging energy with the world outside and also inside itself. The cells of the plants—like your seaweed here—are contained in solid envelopes somewhat different from ours, and the envelopes have special grains which take in energy directly from the sunlight and which give them their colour of green. You and I both eat these plants in order to acquire that energy, and with the aid of the oxygen from the air we convert it in turn into energy of our own, which we later discharge in our movements. We humans eat not only plants but, like your hawks, other animals as well, and thus lay in the energy of the sun at third hand instead of at second. You and I and the seaweed are situated, with a great many other creatures, on the surface of a large solid mass of molecules of the crystallized sort, which is nearly a thousand times as big around as this little island is long—a body with a rocky crust and, presumably, an iron core, which is almost a sphere like the sun, as it looks to us when it sets in the sea but somewhat caved-in on four faces, in which have collected the oceans. The earth has caved-in in this fashion because it is giving off energy, and, as it does so, its atoms are crowding together, and, as they do so, the earth is shrinking. It is roundish because it is revolving. It is revolving steadily about the sun, which is a million and three hundred times as large as it, and it is accompanied by seven bodies of varying size but similar shape. They are moving, as do the electrons around their centres, in a series of successive rings— except that in the case of this system there is only one body in each ring, that each body continues in its course, without shifting from one orbit to another, and that all of the courses lie flat like a wheel. The sun itself is spinning in space, and these other bodies are fragments broken off from it—as the moon is, in turn, from our earth. The planets go around the sun and the moon around the earth in this way, because space is somehow warped in the vicinity of matter, and, in following a curve in this fashion, they are taking what is for them the straightest possible path, from which, once they have been set in motion, it is impossible for them to depart. The laws of their movements are known to me, and I am able to predict their behaviour. In the space where they perform these evolutions, we are not aware of molecules or atoms —our air is only a film about the earth—but of a medium different from those we know, incapable of being analysed into parts but through which energy is able to pass in the form of heat and light. As the sun and our companions, the planets, cool down, they are contracting in the same way as the earth; and, if they continue, will no doubt some day be all as cold and dead as the moon, which goes on falling in its little orbit like a bleaching bit of bone. The sun, however, holds up still and, where the atoms are in violent agitation, is sending out energy at a terrific rate. We on earth depend upon it for energy : we have so little left of our own. It is the sun which now gives us life. Outside the small and limited system in which we find ourselves, we can see half a million more systems apparently in different stages of the process through which our own has passed or in stages through which it will later pass, and a hundred million suns or more, some of them supposed to be a hundred million times as bright as our own sun is. These systems have collected in a larger system which has somewhat the shape of this watch of mine and in which our own system is situated slightly above the middle and close to one end. All these systems are evidently moving in relation to one another, but we do not know precisely how : so far as we can see, our own is headed at top speed towards a certain group of distant suns. This enormous inclusive system is probably moving as a unit itself and absorbing stars on the way. As for the space in which all this is happening, it is natural to think of it as boundless, but, though one could no doubt travel through it without ever arriving at a limit, we have reason to believe it is self-contained, that there is only a certain amount of it, and that the impression we have of infinity is an illusion that is quite nonsensical. *(He tweaks the Iguana's tail.)* I see you are sound asleep and have not listened to a word I have been saying. Yet it has given me gratification, in face of your brutish indifference, to run over all I know.

THE IGUANA *(waking up)*. Not at all : I have enjoyed it much. The gentle ebb and flow of your voice like the surf against the shore, has had a soothing effect on my spirit, and the refrains which recurred from time to time added a refinement of rhythm. You were humming a song when you first came up, and I noticed the same pleasant qualities. Both were delightful expressions of the rhythm which we all feel—in eating, in breeding, in breathing. Ah, that is the basic thing—rhythm, my friend, rhythm !

THE ZOOLOGIST. I gave you, then, no new vision of the universe?

THE IGUANA. From what you had said I was under the impression that you were going to elucidate a mystery; but in the little I listened to before I fell asleep I observed that you were basing your universe upon mysteries even more extraordinary than those I had begged you to accept. What, in fact, are those electrons you speak of, and what makes them rush about so? What, precisely, is that energy they release? I am totally unable to imagine it.

Electrons, if they move in that way, must be living creatures like ourselves, and, therefore, incomprehensible. But whereas I had formerly supposed that only the animals were living things, you seem to want to convince me that everything is. I do not, furthermore, find it possible to imagine the behaviour of beings which first whirl about in one orbit, then suddenly appear in another. Such a conception is against my experience. When the birds I see flying above me come down to the earth or the sea, they do so in an unbroken descent—they do not make the drop instantaneously. I do not understand why you sneer at the man who was content with the mystery of the tiger when you seem to be perfectly satisfied with the mystery of the electron. Could you not apostrophize the electron—and with even stronger reason :

> Electron ! Electron ! circling swift,
> Who taught you that tremendous shift?

THE ZOOLOGIST. We do not accept the mystery of the leaping electron. We expect eventually to fathom it. When the first voyagers came to these seas three hundred years ago, they called this archipelago "the Enchanted Islands," because they were under the illusion that they vanished and reappeared. It was simply that they still knew so little about calculating distances at sea that they were sometimes, without being aware of it, carried out of their courses by strong currents and believed that they were sailing over places where the islands have been formerly seen. That is, they attributed to a mysterious power a phenomenon of which they had simply not yet discovered the true explanation. And that is the type of all scientific progress. Today, our electrons which disappear from one orbit and instantaneously appear in another are inexplicable like the Enchanted Islands, which were sometimes there and sometimes not. But we have found out the secret of the islands and we may find out the secret of the electron. As for what makes the electrons move, science has never pretended to deal with ultimate realities. We leave that to mystics like you. It is enough for us to know *how* they move. All that we scientists pretend to understand are the natural relations involved in the processes of living bodies as well as the natural relations in the processes of the non-living world. People used to imagine that life could spontaneously come into being—again, like the Enchanted Islands. They talked of bees springing to life in the carrion of dead animals and of mice being generated by a piece of cheese and a pile of dirty rags; but now we have found out that what were thought to be bees are not bees but the kind of flies that breed in decaying flesh, and we know how the flies and mice got there just as we know how the islands got there. Who knows if we may not in time come to understand their genesis so well that we shall be able to construct bees and mice ourselves from their component energy and atoms? We have already, as a matter of fact, made impressive beginnings in this direction. Already we have produced out of non-living substances artificial cells that look like real ones and that move, eat and multiply exactly as if they were alive; we have caused artificial seeds to sprout and grow leaves and stalks like those of water-plants. Already we have succeeded in producing a substance called formaldehyde—which is one of the systems of molecules built up by plants and has always been regarded as inseparable from living organisms—by passing a non-living salt through a gas in the presence of rays of sunlight; and by mixing certain crystals with certain liquids we have even brought into being the little furry and living organisms called moulds. We have kept a piece of animal tissue alive, by feeding it its accustomed diet, for five years after the rest of the body was dead. We have determined the sex of pigeons before they were hatched, and have fertilized the eggs of frogs by pricking them with a needle. We have stimulated the ova of sea urchins to develop into eggs and even hatch by supplying them artificially with the requisite enveloping membrane that had formerly been contributed by the male!

THE IGUANA. Indeed? Well, I really cannot see what is the use of taking all that trouble. There is always an abundance of water-plants. I have never known the supply to give out; and I am sure they reproduce themselves a good deal more satisfactorily than you could produce them in that difficult way. As for mice, I cannot imagine why anyone should want them at all!

THE ZOOLOGIST. We do not really need more mice; yet we have our use for such little creatures. Through our work with them, we hope to learn how to reconstruct human beings. They are more useful to us than you may think. By breeding, for example, our ordinary mice with the kind that have the habit called "waltzing," we have been able to ascertain exactly the mathematical proportion according to which they inherit this habit, and thus have come to hope that we may some day be able to trace the inheritance of our own characteristics. Furthermore, from experimenting with the embryos of rats we have concluded that it may become possible to gestate human embryos outside the womb and so do away with the hardships of pregnancy and giving birth, which among us human mammals are so much greater than among you iguanas, who have developed a natural device for growing your offspring outside the body. May we not hope some day to discover, among the bodies of the germinal cell, the sources of the various qualities exhibited by human beings? May we not hope to fertilize the ova, and to rear the embryo, outside the womb? And may we not, then, succeed in cultivating those qualities we regard as valuable and eliminating those we don't want? May we not, in short, some day attain the skill to breed virtue and genius in men as we already breed waltzing in mice?

THE IGUANA. I cannot understand this passion for changing yourselves. Aren't you good enough the way you are? I am sure that, for my part, it would never occur to me to tinker with iguana nature—it is perfectly satisfactory already.

THE ZOOLOGIST. No: from our own point of view, we human beings are not satisfactory. We are rarely content with ourselves or comfortable in our situations. In the first place, we often live in climates where there is so little food available that we are compelled to the extremity of labour in order to get enough to eat, and where the weather is so unfavourable that we are forced to build elaborate shelters and to wear artificial skins. Those who do not care to raise for food animals and plants of their own or to make their own houses and clothing—and of these there are an enormous number—must perform other kinds of labour in order to earn enough precious metal to exchange for these basic necessities; and they tend to huddle in large close communities, which remind one of those of the ants and bees, except that they are not so well organized; for they have never found any stability but are always plunging back and forth between a miserable state of things where there is not enough work to go round and many must beg or

starve and furious spells of activity in which their industries are
overproducing and, in many cases, multiplying commodities that
are ill-made, unnecessary or positively noxious. Our cities, furthermore, are so densely built, so befogged with the gases from our
workshops, that they have ended by excluding the sunlight, upon
whose energy all life depends—as the result of which our city
populations are both overworked and undersunned. But we are
naturally so ill-adapted to the conditions under which we must
live—let alone these artificial ones—that we are continually falling
victim to ailments—insanities, deformities, depletions—caused by
our failure to cope with these. And there are also the contagious
infections : we dwell among a poisonous race of invisible plantlike
creatures which are always lying in wait to devour us when any
weakness on the part of our tissues allows them an opportunity.
With all these annoyances and dangers, we have become more
quarrelsome than ants and continually make war on each other,
collectively and individually, and sometimes on so great a scale
that whole races attack one another for some valuable source of
fuel or food or materials for manufacture until both have destroyed
in the struggle more value in materials and human life than they
could ever have sacrificed by surrendering its object. Now we
scientists—aside from such methods of what we call biological
experiment as I spoke of a moment ago—are developing also
special techniques for dealing with these misfortunes. We study
the nature of plants with a view to producing artificially the substances for which we are dependent on them, in the hope of
making our nourishment as abundant and as easily accessible to us
as your seaweed is to you. We have also what we call social
sciences, which study our complex communities with a view to
producing stability by a redistribution of money and food. We
have a science which works on the mind and attempts to straighten
out the sad tangles that result from our frequent inability—
constrained and imprisoned as we often are by our family and
social relations—to satisfy our natural desires, for mating, for the
kind of work that we like or simply for relaxation. Another sort
of scientific specialist hunts down the bacteria which prey on us
and discovers weapons against them. Still another is a master of
the remedies for stimulating our organs when they fail us and

purifying them when they are poisoned. Another, when these organs are out of order, has learned how to take them apart and repair them and set them running properly again; to graft upon us fresh organs or tissues taken from other bodies, when our own have been injured or torn away, and to supply us, when drained of our blood, with new blood from other arteries. A fourth, by application of energy in the form of certain rays, is able to readjust the atomic structure of our bodies when this has ceased to function in a normal fashion. Unfortunately, we are also the victims of a widespread stupidity which is also infectious. This is probably our most serious plague of all, for it leads us to use our inventions as instruments for our own undoing. Out of our knowledge of molecules and atoms and our mastery of what we call energy, we have created the machines that make it possible for us to do many wonderful things but that also enslave and strain us, and new weapons of unprecedented power to annihilate ourselves by the million. But even this we may in time find remediable. Already we have learned the trick of advancing the idiotic to a relatively normal mentality by stimulating certain secretions which we have found in the recesses of our bodies. Who knows if we may not soon raise the normal to a condition approaching intelligence?

THE IGUANA. The more you go on talking like that, the plainer it becomes to me that you men are mistaken. The further you proceed along such lines, the worse off you are certain to be. Your misfortune really lies, not in knowing too little and in not having arranged things enough, but in ever having embarked on researches which are obviously doomed to be incomplete, and in attempting to tamper with the principle of life when you do not really understand it. What you need is to return to the natural state—from which you should never have departed. What gives you your belief, for example, that before you have stimulated the rest of your race to think the same thoughts that you think and to see their salvation in the same terms as you—which seems to me in itself unlikely—they will not already have destroyed your whole breed, in one of those wars you speak of? In the meantime, in any case, you fall sick; you starve; you die before your time; you are, you say, always unhappy. Such things never happen to us. We follow the decrees of Nature and we are never troubled by "tangles"—whatever you mean by that—which result from the repression of our natural desires. We enjoy ourselves, we mate, we relax. In the morning, in our comfortable burrows, we wake up with the waking of light; then we lie on some favourite rock till the waters have withdrawn from the seaweed; then we saunter down to the shore and munch it fresh from the surf—how delicious and slimy and cool! Then all day, as you see us here, we bask in the luscious sun. Why not yield to this warm old Nature? Loaf and love as we lizards do! You talk a great deal, like the birds; but it is plain from your own description that—whatever you may think—your objects are primarily the same as theirs and mine : to get enough to eat, to enjoy the sun, to perpetuate your kind. If your country, as you say, is sunless, if there is not enough nourishment there, I advise you to move to our country, where there is room for so many more. But, if you do, kindly leave us alone. Do not try to put us together differently; do not stimulate our secretions. You would only distress us and make us ill. Our iguana nature has never changed, and we do not want to have it change!

THE ZOOLOGIST. Has it not? I have seen the skeletons of lizards twenty times the size of the largest lizard now in existence! They were obviously the offshoots, in the distant past, of some ancestor you have in common. Would you tell me in the presence of those gigantic skeletons—articulated exactly like your own—that your nature has never changed? I could show you at the top of my own brain the last useless vestige of an eye which no longer functions for me, but which still survives in you to the degree that one can still see its retina and lens on a scale in the middle of your forehead : if I pass my hand, when you are sleeping, between this open eye and the light, you are aware of it and wake up at once; and I could show you in the embryos of both our kinds the gill-clefts of the water-breathing beings from which we have both descended! What sort of a creature was I when I, too, had an eye in the middle of my forehead? What sort of a creature were you when you lived in the water and breathed through gills? We were not yet a man and a lizard. We were perhaps the same creature then. Have we not immensely changed since that time? You are right—we do share the same nature; but it is proper to

that nature' to change! Your ancestors developed into dinosaurs
—that is, they became huge and strong—and they must have had
the mastery of their animal world. But then, when the climate
turned cold, their strength could not help them to cope with it,
and they perished every one. Now, we men, when in turn we
took flight from a different stock from yours, worked out more
effectual means for dealing with the treacheries of the globe. We
became, not so strong as the dinosaurs, but skilful with our brains
and hands—we elaborated techniques for the use of tools. A few
of the other animals had developed some knack at this; but, for
the most part, you had never got beyond the stage of *growing*
the instruments you needed as attachments to your bodies themselves—your knives, your wings, your oars, your lights, your diving-
helmets, your storage batteries, your weapons to defend yourselves
and your baits to inveigle your prey. To produce such devices as
these must have taken you millions of years, and the number that
one animal can manage is bound to be very limited. But we humans
have learned how to make them from the materials we find to
hand : we can avail ourselves of tools without number, because
they are separate from us—we can pick them up when we need
them and afterwards put them away. And this cleverness may
carry us far. I told you that we were always maladjusted; but our
capacity for adapting ourselves to all kinds of unfavourable conditions that we never were intended to meet is perhaps the most
remarkable triumph that our human breed has yet achieved. We
can survive in more kinds of environment than any other creature
that has ever lived. Yet we must work at our tools day and night.
And that is the scientist's task. There are men who are content
like you to eat and sleep in the sun, to cultivate the enjoyment
of their appetites and to look forward no further than their own
extinction, or to rest serene in their confidence in the instincts
which stir us so confusedly and in the energy which may sweep
us to destruction as easily as to creation and joy; but the scientist
knows that his race can only improve itself, can only make its
works endure, through the power of abstract thought and the
construction of subtler machines—lest we be caught by some new
trick of Nature or some perverse kink of our own before we are
ready to deal with it, and the conquest of living tissue and in-

organic matter be all to begin again by some other race of beings, while, it might be, degenerate members of our own, all their high ambitions run out, would live on to stare at the process, as you lizards, in stupid indifference, watch us men sail the seas and fill in the swamps where your family was once unchallenged. Not the artist nor the saint shall save us, but the scientist—for he alone can perform the calculations and manipulate the tools. The artist and the saint, like him, must chafe at their existence on this difficult earth where they are masters and yet partly helpless. Like him, they hear the voice which torments us : "What we are is not good enough! What we are doing is not good enough!" But the artist can project his chagrin into the beauty of a work of art and so be relieved of it for ever; and the saint can find peace in the hope that what we lack so distressingly on earth will be made up to us after we leave it. Both, like any iguana, can assert that human nature has never changed and that they would not have it change. But the scientist has seen it change and knows that it must change as much again—as much again and more! *Then, then,* we shall have a real world like the worlds that are dreamed by our poets and saints—a world that has passed not only through man's mind but through his hands, also! In that day, we shall no longer have to comfort ourselves by the makeshifts of our imaginations for the diseases of our minds and bodies and the grounding of our high desires. Inhabiting in that day a universe which will itself be a masterpiece of imagination, the speech that we use in our daily life will become more compact and quick, electrically conveying its meanings, and, exulting in our freedom of power, we shall improvise ephemeral songs beside which the lyrical voices of the Beethovens, the Shakespeares and the Dantes —those cries of maladjustment and pain—will seem almost the stammering of barbarians! And in that day our purest saints would regard it as shame—in their raptures, their visions of the nature of reality—to have had to buy sainthood through suffering!

THE IGUANA. Your Beethovens, your Dantes and your Darwins do not matter in the least to me. It is now growing dark—I must get home to my burrow. (*He begins to crawl away.*)

THE ZOOLOGIST. Yes, our planet, as it wheels us about, hides the sphere of the sun from our eyes; and the light, striking through earth's film, streams divided in purple and green. But you shall not go back to your burrow tonight—you shall come away with me! (*He lassoes the Iguana with a cord.*)

THE IGUANA. Why do you want me to go with you?

THE ZOOLOGIST. You must help me to attain that triumph of which I have just been telling you!

THE IGUANA. If, as you say, the sun is burning out and we all depend upon it for life, where will your triumph be when the sun is as dead as a boulder and the earth as cold as the moon?

THE ZOOLOGIST. Look there! Behind us a million suns are beginning to shine in the eastern sky, all blindingly ablaze like our own. We shall have those down to warm us when our own has given out!

THE IGUANA. That strikes me as a dubious hope—if their sizes are what you represent them. Nothing but a mystic faith, a faith as instinctive as mine, could inspire an idea so unscientific! In that faith, let us go to our beds; let us sleep on the wonderful mystery. There is nothing so comforting in life as slumber in a cosy burrow.

THE ZOOLOGIST. You sleep too much : while we sleep, we acquiesce in the undoing of our children. Since you take no thought for your own, you shall help me to save mine! (*He carries him off by the tail.*)

THE IGUANA. My children will live as I do.

THE ZOOLOGIST. That is the difference between us.

THE IGUANA. I will bite you! I go unwillingly!

IX

Sex

THE PURPOSE of sexual intercourse, and hence of what we call love, is to secure the survival of the human race and, if possible, to improve its breed.

This would seem to be obvious enough, yet I have found, on several occasions, when I have emphasized this truism in conversation, that I have provoked the most vehement protests, and have had a suspicion confirmed that for educated people at the present time this objective has been so far lost sight of that it is hard for them to see "love" in terms of it. The sentimentalities, romanticisms, idealisms that make up so much of modern literature have concealed from such people the pattern and the purpose of the mating of human beings, which is basically identical with those of the mating of the other animals. The male makes a play for the female, competing with other males and attempting to impress the female not only by fighting off these competitors, but also by strutting before her, displaying his accomplishments, his prowess, his charms. The Australian lyre-bird has a whole repertoire of devices for dazzling and amusing the female. He dances, he parades the magnificent tail which he specially grows for this season, he gives brilliant imitations of other birds. Not only does he woo her by these means: he keeps her entertained through her period of setting—lyre-birds, as a rule, lay only one egg, and its hatching seems rather precarious. When he is done with this, he loses his tail and retires into the forest, where he works at learning new numbers for his repertoire. It is possible that, as some believe, an element of what we call the æsthetic is involved in such non-human phenomena as the lyre-bird's virtuosity. His range is remarkable : he can even reproduce such mechanical sounds as the scratch of a saw. He acquires new imitations as a singer acquires new songs. Nor is his mate his only audience. In the off-season, he practises his act on the other deplumaged males. Now, a man in his mating time behaves very much like the lyre-bird, and he does so to achieve the same end : to produce baby human beings, as the lyre-bird to produce little lyre-birds. When the female has been won and impregnated, when the offspring have been hatched or born, the attitude of the father changes. He may apply himself more or less effectually to feeding and protecting his family, but he no longer need strain to please. The biological cycle is now complete, the intensity of passion relieved. It may never recur for the man in connection with that particular woman, or he may like her so much that he woos her again and makes her produce more offspring.

One difference, however, between human life and the life of the lyre-bird is to be found in the much greater frequency with which, in the case of humanity, this cycle becomes frustrated or complicated. It would seem that, in the lyre-bird world, there are actually unhappy males who form in the forest a group by themselves and—as seems to be implied in a report on this bird—engage in homosexual practices. One wonders whether the performance of the lyre-bird male may not sometimes prove so unsatisfactory that it fails to hold the hen to her nest. Yet, relatively effete though the lyre-bird is, he manages, in propagating his species, more easily than the human animal. Even a tomcat, who cannot get the tabby he wants will prowl around her prison for days, and it is plain that he actually suffers from unappeased desire; but eventually he may slake this desire with another female cat. Compare the mating behaviour of any of these non-human creatures with those of the creatures we read about in contemporary imaginative literature. Our novels, our plays and our poetry are concerned to what may seem an appalling degree—may seem so, that is, to persons who have known the completed cycle—with people who are shown as feeling in relation to one another a definite biological attraction yet are prevented from experiencing, or are incapable of experiencing, the full cycle of courtship, fruition, relief. Modern literature has become so addicted to presenting situations of this kind that one cannot always be sure whether its writers are fully aware that the anguish of their lovers arises not merely from estrangements, from not being able to enjoy or to renew the ecstasy of love-making, from being deprived by some obstacle of one another's congenial company, but from the basic biological bafflement of the failure to produce children. And of course there is the complication that one does not want just any children. There is the principle of sexual selection. One wants children by a mate one admires. One wants to produce better children. A conflict between the attractions of different possible mates, a falling-back on a *pis-aller* where something much better was aimed at, may provide a situation that interests. Yet in all this it is rather surprising how frequently the prime motivation—the impulse to propagate—is lost sight of in modern life. The various substitutes for the child-getting cycle to which people are often driven by the codes and neuroses of modern life have come so to preoccupy us that we lose sight of the original process. We have had in modern literature, at various epochs, the doomed guilty passion of the British Victorians and the accepted adultery of the French, the long and uncertain engagements and the rejections of irregular relationships of the James and Howells period in the United States, the glorification of intercourse for its own sake as you get it in D. H. Lawrence, the feminine promiscuity of Edna Millay, the homosexuality of Proust that is really a stunted and embittered form of an intense admiration for women, the adolescent sexuality of Gide that does not much transcend masturbation, the homosexual narcissism of Norman Douglas and the dynamic narcissism of Bernard Shaw, who tries to make his women approximate men and who never went to bed with his wife.

The literature of sexual sterility is, however, as old as Plato, and it is curious to contrast these modern works with the point of view of Saadia Ben Joseph, the tenth-century Jewish teacher, who lived in a part of the world where—among the Greeks and the Arabs—homosexual love was accepted. Saadia was quite puritanical even in relation to women and believed that it was "proper for men to satisfy this appetite only in order to produce offspring."

The difficulties, the agonies and the scandals of the current Platonic love therefore seem to him quite fantastic. He might be dealing with the world of Proust when he deplores the loss of appetite and the failure of "all other functions basic to his well being," "the inflammation and the fainting and the heart throbs and the worry and the excitement and the agitation" experienced by the unlucky lover : "The slavish submission to the object of one's passion and to his retinue, and the sitting at the gates and waiting upon him everywhere"; "and what about the vigils at night and the rising at dawn and the secrecy practised so as not to be surprised in the act, and the deaths one dies whenever one is discovered in one's shame? . . . and what about the murder of the lover or the beloved or of one of their retinue or of both them and those attached to them and of a great many human beings together with them that often results from being madly in love, as Scripture says : *Because they are adulteresses, and blood is on their hands?* (Ezekiel xxiii. 45) . . . This emotional state . . . has its appropriate place only in the relationship between husband and wife. They should be affectionate to one another for the sake of the maintenance of the world, as Scripture says : *A lovely hind and a graceful doe, let her breasts satisfy thee at all times; with her love be thou ravished always* (Proverbs v. 19)." I find it admirable of this stout rabbi to insist upon the straight path of procreation while surrounded by Platonic lovers tying themselves into knots. (The romantic adoration of *women*—which in our own day has resulted in similar antics—was not even imagined in Saadia's world.) The Jews have owed much of their strength to their steady concentration on the family line, their loyalty to the family unit. The only great modern writer who has occupied himself seriously with this unit—James Joyce in *Ulysses* and *Finnegans Wake*—has, it seems to me, on that account, been fashionable rather for the brilliance of his technical innovations than for the family situations that always make the core of his work. A short story by Dorothy Parker—a girl who is hanging in anguish on the ring of the telephone—is, from this point of view, not so far from Proust as either of them is from Joyce, with his middle-aged married people, more or less comfortably mated and bound to one another by their children. This is the reason why critics of *Ulysses* can grasp Molly

Bloom's promiscuity but not her underlying fidelity to Bloom that makes of her a true Penelope, and why students of *Finnegans Wake* are likely to be preoccupied exclusively with the verbal tricks and facets of reference at the expense of the commonplace household whose relationships are being explored.

. . .

This is not, of course, to say that the biologically sterile relationships with which modern literature deals are devoid of importance or interest, or that sexual desires ungratified, or which, gratified, produce no children, may not set off consuming passions or stimulate noble virtues. It is true that there is nothing in the world that can become more completely demoralizing, more wasteful of emotional energy, than a prolonged affair with a married woman; that nothing can be more depressing than the situation of unmarried lovers who are not in a position to marry; that homosexuality is, in every sense, a cul-de-sac. Yet in the world in which we are living the problems of neurotic incapacitation, the shakiness of economic security, the difficulties in a mixed society of living up to principles of sexual selection which must always be to some extent inherited—all these obstacles to procreation must drive many to *pis-allers* which themselves become tests of character and pressures towards "sublimation." Nor should I advocate as a general policy—as Theodore Roosevelt did—that everyone should get married young and beget as many children as possible. These sterile arrangements should be recognized as the *modi vivendi* they are : they ought not to be glorified. The renunciations of Henry James, the hysterical orgasms of Lawrence, the impotent and obsessive suspicions of Proust are all equally sexual monstrosities, dislocations of the reproductive instinct. Yet, for all we know, such states of mind may mark—as extreme symptoms—a period of difficult transition from our previous habits of reproduction to the mastery of new methods, a period in the course of which a continual process of dislocation will give rise to confusion and anguish. I mean that humanity may be reaching a phase in which the improvement of the human breed will no longer be entrusted entirely to our present hit-or-miss practice, to the pairing-off of individuals who at the moment happen to look good to one another.

To the young, such a prospect as this is likely to appear forbidding; but to one who has passed sixty, the exercise of the sexual functions can hardly be made a cult or the longing for it give rise to extravagant idealization. The attainment of this satisfaction can no longer present itself as a supremely desired end, as it sometimes does in youth—when, however, we may not be aware that what we are aiming at is offspring more viable than we are. We have not yet arrived, at sixty, at the state of the aged Sophocles, who is made to say, in Plato's *Republic,* that he is glad to have escaped at last from a mad and cruel master. We still may desire, touch rapture, we still may be left as if drunken with the aftermath of love. We may even feel occasional symptoms of falling in love again, as we do those of some old ailment—gout or a sneezing from roses—to which we have become accustomed and which by this time we know how to cure. Yet sex has come to seem more irrelevant to the other things that occupy our minds, and we may sometimes push it away with impatience when we are busy with something else. We do not now want any more children. It is as much as we can do to give adequate attention to those we already have. And at this time of life, in this state of mind, we can just begin to catch a glimpse of a world in which what we call love would be demoted to a place less important than it has occupied for our part of the world in the past. It has never been so important among certain other peoples—with the Japanese, for example— as it is supposed to be in the West. In every country, as a matter of fact, the word *love* means something different. Our American ideal of love has come to us by way of romanticist Europe from the code of the age of chivalry. We depend on it for sexual selection, for the betterment of the human stock. We demand that prospective parents shall be what we call "in love." But that is not the only principle that has been applied to get this result. The predominant practice in Europe was to build up a social group which would aim to breed for certain qualities. Hence the various aristocracies, and the custom—so solidly establish in France—of assigning one's daughter to a good *parti,* no matter how little he might thrill her, who would be certain to carry on the manners and the virtues one prized. There was no question of sexual passion : for that, both the mates could take lovers, who, according to the rules of the game, would try to avoid illegitimate children. Romanticism ran counter to this system, for it championed the exception, the rebel—the rights of sexual passion. But with us in the United States, where the social groups were so much less solid —where the money so often changed hands and the classes were less clearly defined—the ideal of romantic love became the dominating convention. It has always disguised a good deal that is mercenary, prosaic or sordid; and I doubt whether it will last indefinitely. The situations I have mentioned above—in James and Lawrence and Proust—are reductions to absurdity of it; and they may be at the same time, I suggest, the symptoms of an obsolescence, eventually a scrapping, of this ideal. We can no longer depend for breeding on the maintenance of certain families accustomed to certain conditions and marrying only among themselves. That has always been difficult in the United States, and it is becoming equally difficult in Europe, where the levellings and upheavals of war and the impoverishment of the landowning classes have been making it more and more impossible to preserve these groups intact. In Russia, it has quite gone by the board. The old upper classes were exiled, and even under the Soviet régime, the dictator—jealous of power—kept changing, by dismissal or murder, the personnel of the upper ranks, in order to avert the danger of a powerful governing group who might dig themselves in and displace him. It is said that since Stalin's demise there is a tendency for such a group to coagulate and leave to its children its resources as well as its traditions. Such tendencies are bound to appear. They exist in every American town that more or less respects its "first families"; in every African tribe that cultivates a princely caste. But how much scope will they have in the future? How much will they be encouraged?

What I am getting at is that some new technique of breeding will very soon have to be found. The pretensions of the aristocracies, though never entirely justified, were never perhaps completely false; but that road seems forever closed. A possible new method has already appeared in artificial insemination. I find at the county fairs of the dairy country of upstate New York that the

semen of prize bulls is now advertised and sold like any other
agricultural commodity. Nobody worries about the cows, who, in
addition to losing their calves, are deprived of the pleasure of
begetting them. And, as I learn from the English press, the same
kind of thing is sometimes done, in Britain, for human beings.
This is a method which, I do not doubt, will come to be practised
more widely, but always, I should imagine, exceptionally—in the
case of a husband's sterility or a woman's non-marriageability. It
is more probable that the breeding of the future will be managed
through the systematic practice of what used to be called eugenics.
That remarkable prophet John Humphrey Noyes (1811-1886)
founded the Oneida Community in Oneida County, New York,
with the object of producing a better stock by the supervised
interbreeding—"planned parenthood"—of a carefully selected
group. I have heard that the Oneida people were not always satisfied with the partners with whom they had been put to bed, and
that the couples officially paired would sometimes, by mutual consent, escape to other rooms through the transoms and themselves
plan a different parenthood. Yet I do not find it hard to imagine
a movement of this kind in the future, either promoted in some
way by the State or carried out by a private group. Such a movement might well begin with a bureau which should ask for volun-
teers for the breeding of a new élite and which should make a
selection among them based on both intellectual and physical
equipment. I do not believe that such unions would necessarily be
entered into as coldbloodedly as might be supposed. The very ideal
of a new élite would act as a stimulus to enthusiasm—I assume
that, among these recruits and the children produced by their
breeding, there would be time for acquaintanceship and freedom
of choice. We have already seen something of the kind in the
German Youth Movement of Hitler and the Russian Komsomols.
You may well think the Germans absurd, with their pretensions
to Aryan purity, and the Komsomols naïve and priggish. But
unless some such new principle is introduced, I do not know how we
are going to be saved from the dominance of mediocrity and from
a letting-down of all standards with the exception of the mechanical
and technical ones which are necessary for our engineering and in
which a kind of mass training seems possible. The republican and

socialist centuries have insisted on equality of opportunity; but, assuming a civilization where everyone does enjoy equal rights—to employment, to education, to justice before the law, to do what he can with his life—this would certainly not be enough. Equality is not enough, and is, besides, only possible in the limited sense of the kind of rights mentioned above. There is always the drive to excel. Work, literacy, food and shelter, hygienic conditions of living are minimum requirements of civilization, but they will not appease this ambition.

It seems to me, therefore, inevitable that the future will see a great movement for the betterment of the race by breeding. Think what we have done with dogs. Think what we have done with horses. Think what, since Neanderthal man or beginning whenever you like—by methods of deliberate discipline and selection that has been half-conscious—we have already done with the human race. Do not say that you turn in distaste from a selection so calculated and conscious, which does not depend on "the heart." In how many marriages and liaisons in the society we actually inhabit does no calculation enter or the heart play a cardinal rôle?

X

The Author at Sixty

I HAVE LATELY BEEN coming to feel that, as an American, I am more or less in the eighteenth century—or, at any rate, not much later than the early nineteenth. I do not drive a car and rather dislike this form of travel—I have not progressed further than the bicycle. I cannot abide the radio—though I regularly play the phonograph, which gives me, as the radio cannot, exactly what music I want at exactly the moment I want it. I have rarely watched a television programme, and I almost never go to the movies (a word that I still detest as I did the first time I heard it). I have ceased to try to see at first hand what is happening in the United States, and my movements are all along a regular beat, which enables me to avoid things that bore or annoy me. I live mainly in two old-fashioned country towns : Wellfleet, Massachusetts, and Talcottville, New York, with visits of days, weeks or months to New York City and Boston, where I see my old friends and transact my business, and occasional excursions to Washington, Charlottesville and Princeton. I do not want any more to be bothered with the kind of contemporary conflicts that I used to go out to explore. I make no attempt to keep up with the younger American writers; and I only hope to have the time to get through some of the classics I have never read. Old fogeyism is comfortably closing in.

Life in the United States is much subject to disruptions and frustrations, catastrophic collapses and gradual peterings-out. I have felt myself at times, when younger, threatened by some such fate;

but now, in my sixy-first year, I find that one of the things that most gratify me is the sense of my continuity. It seems to me at moments extraordinary that I should still be sitting here in the country—having grown up in country houses, I have always, after spells in the city, come back to the country again—surrounded by the books of my boyhood and furniture that belonged to my parents. I see, on the tops of the bookcases, among my other animals and my Mexican gods, a plaster reproduction of a gargoyle that I bought at Notre Dame at the age of thirteen and a yellow stuffed bird of cloth, most elaborately embroidered with blue and orange beads, that a cousin and I, at an earlier age, bought from an Indian woman on a steamer-trip up the St. Lawrence River, as a present for our Grandmother Kimball, who pleased us by thinking it amusing and hanging it on the gas-jet in her bedroom, to which she was then confined. The bird held a cluster of cherries, also adorned with beads, and one of these cherries has been lost; the gargoyle has lost part of a wing. But it reassures and rather surprises me to find them still with me here, and to know that through all my experiences, different interests, different women, different homes, I can still recognize myself as authentically the same individual who climbed the steep spiral of Notre Dame and who took that trip through the Thousand Islands.

This book was begun in Talcottville in the middle of last August, and I am finishing it here in June. The house in which I am living, which belonged to my family and which now belongs to me, was built out of the local limestone at the end of the eighteenth century. We used to spend the summer in Talcottville. The family reunion in the old town in summer was still at that time a feature of American life in the East, particularly perhaps in New York State. With the further opening up of the West, the families of New York State became widely dispersed, and such places were *points de repères*, they had a unifying and stabilizing function. As my own generation grew up and the older generations died off, we did not return to Talcottville so often. It was dull for us, we wanted to circulate; yet I sometimes came up here alone, when I found nothing better to do, spending weeks of unbroken reading and taking a long walk or a swim in the river every afternoon. I had always the highest regard for my Lewis County relatives. I had grown up in Red Bank, New Jersey, in a town about four miles from the ocean, at a time when that part of the Jersey coast was a resort of, in general, the second-rate rich, and I had passed my prep school years in Pottstown in the midst of the Pennsylvania steel mills. I knew that the Lewis County people—with their dairy farms and big tracts of land in the foothills of the Adirondacks—had a dignity and a self-assurance that many Americans lacked. They were amiable, calm, independent. I have been fortified by this place and its people to withstand many fakes and distractions. And now that I have seen the world, I no longer find them dull.   .   .   .

The period after the Civil War—both banal in a bourgeois way and fantastic with gigantic fortunes—was a difficult one for Americans brought up in the old tradition : the generation of my father and uncles. They had been educated at Exeter and Andover and at eighteenth-century Princeton, and had afterwards been trained, like their fathers, for what had once been called the learned professions; but they had then had to deal with a world in which this kind of education and the kind of ideals it served no longer really counted for much. Such people, from the moment they left their schools, were subjected to dizzying temptations, overpowering pressures, insidious diversions of purpose, and the casualties among them were terrible. Of my father's close friends at college, but a single one was left by the time he was in his thirties : all the rest were dead—some had committed suicide. My father, though highly successful, cared nothing about making a fortune or keeping up with current standards of luxury, which in our part of the world were extravagant. Like many Americans who studied law, he had in his youth aimed at public life, and a letter to my mother from Exeter, written in 1880—when she was a student at Abbot Academy—encloses a newspaper clipping which reports the visit to the school of a Republican candidate for governor : "Those Phillips Academy boys," the reporter declares, "looked just splendid; there must be several future governors among the lot and good stock for a President." At Princeton he was famous as an orator, in the days of an active Whig Hall. But the political career he had hoped for was conceived in the classical republican terms.

After law school, he went as a delegate to one of the Republican conventions, and he continued to follow politics, to advise the Republican party and sometimes to make campaign speeches; but —though he did not lack encouragement to run for office—he could not beyond this be induced to take any active part in the kind of political life that he knew at the end of the century. By the time he was thirty-five, he was subject to neurotic eclipses, which came to last longer and longer and prove more and more difficult to cope with. He suffered from hypochondria—the only neurosis which, according to Freud, the analyst cannot touch; and there were in those days no analysts : the system of Weir Mitchell prevailed. Such conditions were called neurasthenia. Dr. Mitchell had grasped the fact that the speeded-up pace of American life, the constant changing-hands of money which produced social insecurity in a society where social position was coming more and more to depend on money, were driving Americans to overwork and to anxieties that became obsessive—*obsession* was one of the words that loomed large in my father's vocabulary. Weir Mitchell invented the "rest cure," where people got away from their worries. My father spent all of his later years in and out of these sanatoriums. But before he had got to this point, he had been sent to a "neurologist" in London by one of my mother's physician brothers, who had made him go abroad, I think, in order to get him away from his work. My mother, as a young woman—so her maid of over fifty years tells me—did not seem to "have a nerve in her body"; but the effect on her of my father's derangement must have been deeply shocking. On the boat she became deaf— literally overnight—and never regained her hearing. When the doctor in London had examined my father, he saw my mother alone and said, "Your husband is mad." This upset my mother but made her indignant, since she knew he was not really mad. The next device tried by my uncle was himself to take my father to Carlsbad and to have him sit at outdoor cafés, listening to Lehar waltzes and consuming much Pilsener beer. The effect of this treatment was excellent. My father became quite cheerful and no longer imagined he was dying of one illness after the other. I believe that his hypochondria may partly have been a form of the Calvinist fear of damnation. I have spoken of my formidable grandmother, who had also, my mother told me, a "queer" and morbid side. And my father had undoubtedly been frightened as well as severely taxed by the fate of his only brother, who—a milder personality, much loved, rather more on the literary side, with less energy and authority than my father—had not survived his thirty-eighth year. My Uncle John had studied law at the University of Virginia and had married the daughter of the head of the school, a delightful Virginian woman, full of humour and charm, with no grasp of practical life and—aside from a trip to Europe and occasional visits in the East—with little experience of any society outside the old-fashioned Virginian one. My Uncle John took her to Pittsburgh, where he had a few friends from college and where he supposed there were great opportunities. They had three handsome children there. But Pittsburgh was too much for my uncle and aunt. I remember a description of them by someone who had seen them then : the young husband lying on his back on a couch, so ill that he could not practise, the young wife—so I imagine, though I am told she would never hear a word against Pittsburgh—quite out of her element with the Pittsburghers and the cold Western winter. He was found to have Bright's disease, and they could not go on any longer. She returned to her family in Charlottesville, taking the three children. He went to stay with his parents, who were then at Spring Lake, New Jersey. That was the winter and the blizzard of 1899. My uncle grew rapidly worse, and my father came on to Spring Lake, but could not get a doctor on account of the snow. My Aunt Susan had been summoned from Charlottesville. She found a "stage" at the station that would take her to the house, and on the way she heard one of the passengers say, "Such a sad thing about that young man, the son of Dr. Wilson. He's left a wife and three little children, and she wasn't even with him when he died." My father had been there alone with him, unable to do anything for him—the experience was to leave with him a kind of "trauma." And thereafter, only just established, he was obliged to meet the expenses of his brother's family as well as support his own. He was admirable in all this. He was fond of my Aunt Susan, and I never heard him complain of her carelessness in spending money or her tendency to run up debts. He would descend periodically on Charlottesville, sometimes taking me, and straighten out her affairs. She would entertain him lavishly, with relays of "hot bread," Southern fashion, and she would always make him laugh a good deal—undoubtedly one of the most beneficent things that it was possible for anybody to do for him.

Another factor, however, which laid him open to neurotic depressions was his lack of objectives in life. He had given up political ambitions; he had had every possible success at law, and law in the long run bored him. More and more he would drop his practice and retire to a sanatorium or to a plantation in North Carolina or shut himself up at home in a room with a felt-covered door. When he felt that the money was running low, he would emerge from his shadow or exile and take on a couple of cases, enough work to retrieve the situation. He was a crack trial lawyer, and, in the latter part of his life, was much sought after by other lawyers to try their less easy cases. He had only lost one case in his life, very early in his legal career. He sometimes worked for corporations, who paid him substantial fees; but all kinds of local people would come to him with their troubles, and if he thought that they had been badly treated and had a good case, he would rescue them from their difficulties for little or nothing. He had got his clients acquitted in several much-publicized murder cases, and I once drove with him to the prison in Freehold, to which he went at the request of a tailor indicted for killing his wife. I could not get him to talk about this interview except to tell me, as we were driving back, that he could not do anything for the man. He had prosecuted only one murderer. The reason for his success was undoubtedly that he never undertook a case which he did not think he could win, and that his judgment about this was infallible. In court, he attacked the jury with a mixture of learning, logic, dramatic imagination and eloquence which he knew would prove irresistible. He would cause them to live through the events of the crime or supposed crime, he would take them through the steps of the transaction, whatever this was, and he would lodge in their heads a picture that it was difficult for his opponent to expel. I was impressed by the intense concentration that these feats of persuasion cost him—they could not be allowed to fail—on the occasions when he prepared a brief at home. He would pace back and forth through the rooms, go nervously up and down stairs, and all other operations would have to be suspended. The atmosphere became insupportable.

Edmund Wilson—I was a Junior—had always been an active Republican but had never held any kind of office till, in 1908, he was appointed Attorney General by a Republican governor of New Jersey. The Democrat Woodrow Wilson, however, succeeded this governor in office before the end of my father's term. My father did not much like Wilson, but to me he was then a great hero. I arrived as a freshman at Princeton when he was still in residence there, and when the college was still divided into passionate adherents and venomous foes. My father took no sides in this controversy, for he did not like Andrew West, the antagonist of Wilson, either. But I read and listened to Wilson's speeches and accepted him as a shining champion in the war against sordid business, a reformer-intellectual in politics. I did not find his literary style quite so excellent as some people thought—it was better to hear him than to read him—but he did have a literary style, which was hardly possible to say of any other recent candidate for the presidency. I would, therefore, when my father at dinner would mention that he had been to see the Governor that day, express an extreme interest. "What is he like?" I would ask, and would receive some such dampening reply as, "He was like an animated corpse." It was only years later that I saw the point of my father's adverse comments on the bigotry and suspiciousness of Wilson. I remember his telling me with amusement of the plaints of the machine politicians who had put Woodrow Wilson in power and had then been repudiated by him with accents of reprobation. No political betrayal of the kind had ever occurred in New Jersey. "I p-picked him," had said one of them, stuttering, "I p-picked him, and I p-picked a lemon!"

Woodrow Wilson had assumed characteristically that my father —allied with his political opponents—was also a member of the Republican machine, and he tried to embarrass my father by demanding that he investigate Atlantic City, a huge Republican racket, which he imagined my father would not dare to touch. Edmund Wilson had no inhibitions, having given no political hostages, and he at once came to grips with the problem, which proved to be tough indeed. The city was run by a boss, who kept his apparatus in power by every species of corruption at the polls; but it seemed at first out of the question to get anyone convicted of anything, since everyone in Atlantic City was either in on the racket or intimidated by the machine. My father then hit upon a brilliant device. He dug out a very ancient New Jersey law that no one else had ever heard of, which—the converse of a change of venue—made it possible for the prosecutor, in cases where a fair trial could not be obtained, to bring in jurors—called elisors—from another county. He thus secured his elisors and tried before them, I think, several hundred men, all or most of whom were sent to jail. He even got a verdict against the boss. He did not dislike this man, and told me that he had behaved with dignity, calmly going off to jail in a fur coat and limousine. My father pointed out to me at this time that—though Wilson undoubtedly did not know it—most of the cities in the United States were controlled by a boss and by methods exactly like those in Atlantic City, and that Atlantic City itself would be back, before very long, in the same situation as before. In the course of these proceedings, the local powers had laid all sorts of traps for my father in the hope of getting something on him, and he had had to fight off several beautiful blondes whose mission was to compromise him. Woodrow Wilson, when the clean-up was accomplished, was so much impressed by this feat—which my father regarded as futile—that when he very soon moved up to the presidency, he kept offering my father appointments. Edmund Wilson, who had never in his life voted anything but the Republican ticket, departed for once from his principles when Wilson ran for president the second time, and voted for the Democratic candidate, for the reason that Wilson, in his speeches, had pledged himself to "keep us out of war"—an act which he afterwards regretted when the President immediately plunged us in. My father did some war work, at Wilson's request, in straightening out the affairs of the sequestrated North German Lloyd, but he would not accept any appointment. Moving to Washington seemed too much trouble, and it would upset his independent habits, for he chose his own tasks and times, and sometimes, as I have said, fell into complete inertia. He would never, for similar reasons, accept offers of partnerships in New York firms. He did not like to specialize; he practised a variety of kinds of law; and he liked to be able to choose his cases. He had had eight years of partnership with an older man and had then, on the latter's death, established himself alone on the floor above a liquor dealer—which was always rather pleasantly permeated by a casky vinous smell—from which he continued to operate all the rest of his life. But one day when we were taking a walk he told me, with an injunction of secrecy, that the President had sounded him out as to whether he would fill the next Supreme Court vacancy. This, he felt, would be interesting enough to reconcile him to living in Washington, and he had said that he would accept. But no vacancy occurred during Wilson's term. My father died not long after this—in 1923, in his sixty-first year.

He followed the eccentric—perhaps unique—course, for a public man in New Jersey, of never investing in anything. He regarded the Stock Exchange as a gambling house, and he did not approve of gambling. This gave him a tremendous advantage in a state that was dominated by corporations. Since he did not have a stake in anything, he was quite free to act as he pleased. At the memorial unveiling of a portrait of him in the courthouse of the county seat, Freehold, it happened that the eulogy of him was read by the lawyer brother of a great public utility family, and he frankly confessed his perplexity at sometimes having found my father on the opposite side from himself in cases that involved corporations. My father was at one time attorney for the Pennsylvania Railroad, as well as later on a member of the New Jersey Board of Railroad Commissioners, and he had grown to loathe the P.R.R. Once when I was away at school, my mother sent me a box which contained a few clothes, a cake and several volumes of Shakespeare. It arrived with the package broken open, the clothes and the *Hamlet* gone and the chocolate cake considerably battered. My father proceeded with glee to bring a suit against the Pennsylvania Railroad, and compelled them to pay him damages, regretting that these had to be small. The sole speculation of his life was a shrewd deal in Florida real estate, the future of which he early foresaw.

When I ran down big business, he would answer—as a Republican, he could hardly do less—that the business men had done a good deal to develop our national resources. But business men bored him; and when his classmate Rodman Wanamaker attempted to muster support for his project of a business school at Princeton, he was strongly opposed by my father. He had few companions in Red Bank, none on his own level. He amused himself mainly by travelling. From the moment he arrived in a city, he began asking people questions, beginning with the driver of his cab. It was characteristic of him that he took me once to Salt Lake City. We read up the history of Mormonism and even tried the Book of Mormon, which turned out to be dreadful stuff. He was completely without snobbery of race or class—which was not the case with my mother, who would not allow him to bring some of his friends to the house. He was on very good terms with the Negroes and often spoke to Negro audiences. There was a very large Negro population in Red Bank, with several Negro papers, and it is true that it was important for the Republicans to get out the Negro vote; but his sympathy with them was quite sincere, and he liked to read books about Negro self-advancement, such as those of Booker T. Washington. His closest ally in Red Bank was a Jew from Czechoslovakia, who had come into New Jersey as a pedlar and had built up entirely by himself the sole industry in Red Bank : a uniform factory. This man sent his sons to Harvard, and he and my father were the only people in town who were seriously interested in education. Together, and without much encouragement, they attempted to give Red Bank a first-class school system. They were also, I learn from an obituary, "associated in a number of private and personal charities." My father's benefactions were many and sometimes rather odd. One day I discovered in his library a group of books by a poet of whom I had never heard— old-fashioned Victorian verse of a very insipid kind. This puzzled me, for he never read poetry, and I asked him what on earth they were, expressing my opinion of their quality. I saw that he was rather abashed, since he thought I had some competence in these matters. He murmured that Mr. R. was a very refined old gentleman. I found out later, by asking my mother, that my father had financed these volumes. He also financed a young man who had been working as a sign-painter in Red Bank but who wanted to become an actor. He got more pleasure out of this investment than he did from the works of the poet. The young man, in a certain field, turned out to be a great success. He built up a travelling stock company that was one of the most popular in the East. Yet it always remained something of a mystery why this man should have wanted to go on the stage. It would be wrong to call him a ham, since he had no theatrical abilities of even the coarser kind. He stood about on the stage like a cigar-store Indian, and he had never improved his English to the point of being able to deliver grammatical lines correctly. But the rest of the company were not so bad : it consistently improved with time and included one or two at least respectable actors. Whenever C.K.C. came to Red Bank, my father would go two or three nights a week. He always sat in the front row at the theatre, and there, under the nose of his protégé, he would chuckle with delight at the absurdities of the dramas and the ineptitudes of the leading man. He was pleased by the latter's success, and he regarded the whole thing a little as a show he had arranged for his own entertainment. He loved to quote lines from these plays. One of his favourite scenes occurred in some melodrama of London high life. Sir Charles is saying something that agitates the hero deeply; he manifests this agitation by a few stiff and jerky gestures. "Why, what is the matter?" asks Sir Charles; he has been swinging a pince-nez on a ribbon. "Sir Charles," replies C.K.C., concealing the true reason, "them glasses make me nervous." This actor was much too stupid to be aware of my father's attitude, and he always adored my father, on the occasion of a birthday sending him an enormous framed photograph of himself (my father), with a tribute in gold lettering. After my father's death, when my mother bought a new house, this actor purchased our old one.

I have found among my father's papers a speech on the Homestead strike, in which he sharply takes the strikers to task. This, in the early nineties, was of course the correct Republican line. Having read the Fabian Essays and other socialist writings, I always assumed through my college days that my father was as reactionary as I was advanced, and I did not dare discuss my ideas with him; but I had failed, as I realized later, to understand his real point of view. One of his favourite cronies in Red Bank was the socialist editor of a local paper, and, since my mother would not allow him to invite this man to dinner—she objected to his deliberately unmodish clothes and asserted that he did not wash—they were obliged to take long walks together. It was only after the war when I came back from France, and felt quite independent, that I ventured to talk to my father about socialism in Europe and Russia. To my surprise he was not disapproving, but spoke of it with moderation as something they went in for abroad which had no relevance to the United States. "The main merit of socialism," he said—he was thinking of our local variety—"is to emphasize the brotherhood of man." I was by that time no longer afraid of him, and only then did I get to know him. My first meeting with him on my return unexpectedly made me feel proud of him. I had been waiting for my discharge all too many days in a Long Island army camp, and he came to see me there. He was always impatient of delay, and he complained with his usual peremptoriness to a bureaucratic officer who had failed to produce me at once. The officer had retorted that he'd better be careful, he couldn't talk to the Army like that, there were penalties for that kind of talk. "You're no doubt thinking," my father replied, "of the Espionage Act and the Sedition Act. Neither of them has any application to what I've been saying to you nor to what I'm about to say. The inefficiency of you army people is an outrage against the tax-paying citizens." I was gratified when—still fuming—he told me about this interview: I had had almost two years of the army, and a story I had written in France about the dismal side of army life had recently been held up by the censor when I had tried to send it to the United States, and had brought upon me a bawling-out. When I got home, I was rather surprised—knowing how little my father could sympathize with the aims of the Communists and Anarchists —to find that he was indignant over the arrests without warrant and the indiscriminate expulsion of radicals. I had been so full of Wells and Shaw and Barbusse and the Russian Revolution that I was only learning now from my father what the principles of American justice were.

He enormously admired Lincoln—his allegiance to the Republican party had undoubtedly been partly inspired by this. He collected a whole library of Lincolniana, and he liked to deliver a popular speech called *Lincoln the Great Commoner*. I made, automatically, a point of knowing as little as possible about Lincoln.

I could see that my father in some way identified himself with the Great Commoner, and this seemed to me purely a pose, which verged upon demogoguery. I have said that he was quite without snobbery, but though he dealt with people strictly on their merits, it was always to some extent *de haut en bas*. When he died, I was struck by the criticism in one of the local papers that, in spite of his distinguished qualities, he had either not the desire or the ability to meet people on a democratic level. Both at home and in his office, he was constantly sought by persons who wanted to ask his advice on every conceivable subject, and when he died, many people we had never seen—sometimes poor farmers and their wives—came from miles around to his funeral; yet it was true, I remembered, when I read this obituary, that he had always told people what to do in a dictatorial tone and with a certain restrained impatience, for which, however, he would later try to compensate by dismissing them at the end of the interview with an exaggerated courtesy and sweetness. Where, I wondered, was the kinship with Lincoln? It was only after his death that I understood. Now for the first time I read up Lincoln, and I realized that the biographies he had recommended were always the least sentimental ones. I remembered his saying at a time when he was reading one of the books about Lincoln by Nathaniel Wright Stephenson that it was more realistic than most; and he was always trying to get me to read Herndon—which I never did till after his death. Then, in Herndon's portrait of Lincoln, I at last found the explanation of my father's great interest in him : a great lawyer who was deeply neurotic, who had to struggle through spells of depression, and who—as it followed from this portrait—had managed, in spite of this handicap, to bring through his own nightmares and the crisis of society—somewhat battered—the American Republic.

I assumed, as I have said, that my father and I were at opposite poles in everything, and—since he usually appeared so opinionated—I was always surprised by the sympathy, or rather, perhaps by the judicial detachment, with which, in important decisions, he treated my point of view. After college, before I enlisted, I told him I should like to go to Washington to try my hand at political journalism. "At Princeton," he answered, "you specialized in litera-ture; then you went to Columbia Summer School to study sociology and labour. Now you want to do political journalism. Don't you think you ought to concentrate on something?" "Father," I replied, "what I want to do is to try to get to know something about all the main departments of human thought. I don't know anything about politics yet, and I'd like to see something of it at first hand." He did not even smile at this. "That's a possible ambition," he said. "Go ahead if you're really serious." He had, however, a horror of my not making something of myself—I think he had been appalled by the frivolities of that moneyed era—and he told me from time to time that I was not to be "a rich man's son"—by the standards of that period, we were not very rich—and that he would send me through school and college and give me an allowance for study and travel up to the time I got out of Princeton; but that I would then have to shift for myself. This hung over me all through college as a menace, but he never allowed me to get into serious straits—though, when he died, he did not leave me a penny. Of course, living was easier then. I was almost able to cover my expenses—in an apartment on East Eighth Street, which I occupied with three friends—on the fifteen dollars a week that I drew as a cub reporter; and we were able to keep a Chinese servant and constantly entertained. When my father was sure I was working, he would supplement my pay a little.

My father and my mother had different tastes and temperaments that thwarted one another. My mother was "extroverted," liked bridge-playing, gardening, horses and dogs; she was lively and very shrewd, had no intellectual interests. My father became more and more neurotic; his eclipses, by the time he was fifty, were lasting for months and years, and it was wearing my mother down to try to talk him out of his "symptoms," to amuse him, to arrange for him distractions. His few friends had, in this phase, come to dread him, and he resorted more and more to nurses, who were likely to be a nuisance to my mother, or to the retreats into sanatoriums which completely cut him off from his family. He did not come to my college graduation, and when I went to his sanatorium to see him, he could find nothing whatever to say to me. Through all this I sided with my mother, though I had, I believe, really less in common with her than with my father. It was a case of the only child monopolized by the lonely mother. She had also the impulse to dominate, to manage the people she loved—an instinct of which my father had nothing. He simply gave people advice, did not otherwise try to control them. And I suffered like her from the burden of a chronic depressive in the household. I, too, had to act as companion—to go with him for desolating drives and walks, in the course of which he talked about nothing but his ailments. He studied medical books, and the moment one terror was banished, would discover something even more gruesome. He had already had two operations—which I assume to have been really needed—and the difficulty now was to prevent him from having all his internal organs removed. My mother at one point was on the verge of leaving him. He no longer paid any attention to her, seemed hardly aware of her presence; and she almost convinced herself that he could not be any worse off in the hands of his nurses and doctors. I encouraged her to get away, but she never could take this step. Instead, she had herself a collapse, a slight blood clot which left no bad consequences—she lived to be eighty-six—and which jolted him back for a moment. I remember how touched she was that he was kind to her, solicitous about her. For a moment he forgot his obsessions. I overheard her from my bedroom next to hers ask him whether he no longer loved her, calling him by a nickname that she must have used in their youth—the only time I ever knew her to speak to him in this way; but I do not remember his reply, and, indeed, find it difficult to imagine him answering such a question. Yet he was supposed to have been originally more in love with her than she with him : somebody once told me of his pacing the floor, at a time when her consent was doubtful, and swearing that if she would not have him, he could never marry anyone else.

But, aside from this crisis, which took place at a time when he hardly seemed with us at all, they had serious conflicts of interest even when my father was normal. I remember two major crises, though I cannot remember which came first. They could never agree about travel. My mother wanted to go to places that would be fashionable, lively and gay—the sort of thing that bored my father. Once when she demanded that he take her to the kind of place she liked—I think Florida was in her mind—he planned a trip to Europe that was perfectly irrelevant to her own desires. He had gone ahead and bought passages without asking her approval or, so far as I know, consulting her. One evening, at dinner, she rebelled. She said that she had been travelling with him on his own terms for years, and that there was nothing more in it for her; he simply visited cities, systematically informed himself about their populations, politics and products, inspected their public buildings and looked in on the proceedings of their legislatures, and paid no attention to her. Through his illnesses, he had made it impossible for her to enjoy, even at home, much social life, and when they were travelling, she had no friends at all. His way of taking this surprised me : he resorted to forensic eloquence, reproaching her, in a somewhat grandiloquent way, for having allowed him to go to so much trouble and then capriciously destroying his work. It was as if she had demolished some masterwork, capsized his whole career. I had never before heard him take this line in any situation of private life, and I thought it was due to a conviction of guilt : she had upset a furtive plot. It was the other way around on the other occasion : it was he who sabotaged her plan. When my father and mother were married and first bought the house that we lived in, the eventual prolongation of the Rumson Road was supposed to run past our property; but actually, when the road was completed, it was put through on the other side of the hill at the base of which we lived. Our neighbourhood grew up as a slum. My father made a joke of the slum, but he continually bought more land in order to stave off its encroachment. Our house had been built in the eighties, a bad architectural period, when, for some reason, the rooms of the bottom floor were given enormous doorways and all opened into one another, and when my mother complained of its inconvenience, its inadequacy for the needs of the family, my father would have it enlarged in some way. She decided at last to move and to build another house. We were just off the highways with the big estates, where the rich people were rolling in their shiny black cars, hidden behind our hill, and the capillary attraction to range ourselves with them was strong. My mother had laughed at her sister-in-law, who, in Rumson, had an establishment of the fashionable kind, for her multiplication of servants : she had once taken on an extra maid to answer the telephone; and our household contrasted with hers; no fräuleins and mademoiselles, no turnover of maids and chauffeurs. Most of the members of our staff were permanent. The coachman was the illegitimate mulatto son of a local white judge, so serious and so responsible that he might have been a judge himself. When automobiles came in and we gave up keeping horses, he quietly declined to learn to drive but assumed that he was still in our employ and went on taking care of our single cow, some chickens and a flock of guinea fowl. His wife was part Indian and part Negro—a very handsome woman, proud, taciturn and sometimes fierce; she was our cook, and when anything went wrong in the kitchen, everybody kept away. The main pillar of the household was an Irish girl, who came to work for my parents at the age of sixteen, a few years after they were married. She taught me to walk, and she became indispensable to everyone in the family. She was sensitive, intelligent, affectionate. At one point she decided to leave us and run a boarding house. My father financed her in this, but we got along so badly without her that, at the end of a year or two, he coaxed her into coming back. She was an integral part of the family, knew everything about everybody and everything, and, after my father's death, she continued to stay with my mother and herself handled all the transactions which the deafness of my mother made difficult. This household satisfied my father, but, in spite of her attitude towards my aunt, my mother took on another maid and gave the Irishwoman the title of "housekeeper." We now had to have a chauffeur as well as the non-functioning coachman, and there was also the problem of a gardener. My mother had tried to offset the ugliness and gloom of our house by a blazing and enormous garden, which became more and more of an operation and eventually won first prize in a Monmouth County garden competition. She decided at last that she could not expand any further in our present location, that she must have a new house and new grounds, and she may have persuaded herself that my father had consented to this. She selected an attractive piece of land on one of the transverse roads between the Ridge Road and the Rumson, and she consulted for months with an architect, planning a new habitation in which everything would be exactly as she wanted it. I heartily approved of this—I had no place to work at home where I was not likely to be disturbed by something going on in some other room, and I was not insensible to the luxuries of the Ridge and Rumson Roads—I looked forward to our new demesne. Then one evening, just after dinner, my mother confronted my father with blueprints. He told her in a positive way that he could not afford a new house, that his illness made his income uncertain, and that she would have to put it out of her mind. She knew that he meant it and, in bitter chagrin, she tore up the blueprints in front of him. "The ambition of your Grandmother Kimball," he explained to me a day or two later, "burdened the Doctor's last years. She made him build that new house in Lakewood, and then, when he was old and ill, it was hard for him to keep it up." He added, or implied, that he had made a note not to let that happen to him.

He cared nothing about his surroundings—hence his alcohol-flavoured office, hence the awkwardness of our house. When, after his death, I sometimes slept in his bedroom, I was chilled by its bareness and bleakness : there was nothing but the necessary furniture and photographs of his mother and father. Yet he liked to travel in style and paid a good deal of attention to his clothes. He was tall and good-looking and rather vain, and women were supposed to adore him. He was undoubtedly a very self-centred man, and, when sunk in his neurotic periods, would be shut in some inner prison where he was quite beyond communication. He died of pneumonia; just before he died, he murmured the pathetic question that he had put to us so often about illnesses that were wholly imaginary : "What does the doctor say about my condition?" My mother gave a little cry, but as soon as we had gone downstairs she astounded me by saying immediately, "Now I'm going to have a new house !" She did, not long afterwards, though not on the scale of the one she had originally planned, and when I saw it, I realized fully, and realized for the first time, how much my father had suppressed in her life. Everything about her was suddenly bright. The mahogany and silver shone; the armchairs had flowery covers; there was a sun-parlour full of plants, and large birds with large winged insects fluttering in their beaks appeared on the shades of this sun-parlour. I was reminded of the colour and the smell of my grandmother's house in Lakewood, which was supposed to have been a burden to my grandfather. But my mother then became very sad : she seemed to suffer from the loss of my father as if from an amputation. She would not go near the old house, in which nobody wanted to live and which was soon in a run-down condition; and did not like me to tell her about it when I went there to see what had happened to it.

I had never thought she understood what my father's real point of view was and why, in his professional life, he behaved in the way he did. Her respect for him was partly derived from the respect that other people had for him. Her values were worldly, it seemed to me, to a degree that I sometimes found disheartening : she admired social prestige, and she also admired money. She had had two able brothers with weaknesses of an order somewhat different from my father's—though they were partly due, like his, I believe, to a fundamental lack of adjustment to the American life of the period. She said to me once that "these brilliant men always had something wrong with them." I do not think she was pleased with a destiny that had made her spend her life with such men. And I was another one : she had hoped I would be an athlete, a change from my cerebral father—something more like her sportsman brother who had played on the football team. She was an enthusiastic follower of collegiate sport, and even in her old age she continued as long as she was able to go to football and baseball games at Princeton, and in the off season attended basketball for want of anything better. I was sure that she understood my activities even less well than she did my father's. In the radicalizing thirties, for example, my old friend John Dos Passos took part in a visit of protest to the terrorized Kentucky coal miners and was indicted by a local grand jury under the Kentucky criminal syndicalism law. This had been in the New York papers, and I remember how jarred I was when the next time I saw my mother, she remarked, "I see they've caught Dos Passos." She was sure that Sacco and Vanzetti were "perfectly awful men," who deserved to be executed—though I felt, since she was very kind-hearted, that this was due to her not being able to bear to imagine they had been executed unjustly. Yet I remember, in all this connection, her giving me one touching piece of testimony—entirely unexpected on my part—to her real appreciation of my father. I did not often talk to her about my work, but I did speak to her on one occasion of my fear that I might be outvoted on what I considered some important policy of the liberal weekly for which I wrote. "Your father," she promptly told me, "would go into court when he knew that the judge and the jury were prejudiced, and public sentiment was all against him, and try his case and win it."

.   .   .

My father's career had its tragic side—he died in his sixty-first year. I have been in some ways more fortunate—I am writing this in my sixty-second. And yet to have got through with honour that period from 1880 to 1920!—even at the expense of the felt-muted door, the lack of first-class companionship, the retreats into sanatoriums. I have never been obliged to do anything so difficult. Yet my own generation in America has not had so gay a journey as we expected when we first started out. In repudiating the materialism and the priggishness of the period in which we were born, we thought we should have a free hand to refashion American life as well as to have more fun than our fathers. But we, too, have had our casualties. Too many of my friends are insane or dead or Roman Catholic converts—and some of these among the most gifted; two have committed suicide. I myself had an unexpected breakdown when I was in my middle thirties. It was pointed out to me then that I had reached exactly the age at which my father had first passed into the shadow. I must have inherited from him some strain of his neurotic distemper, and it may be that I was influenced by unconscious fear lest I might be doomed to a similar fate. I did not recover wholly for years, and there were times when I was glad to reflect that I had covered more than half of my threescore and ten—"on the home stretch," I used to phrase it in reassuring myself. But now that I am farther along, I find I want to keep on living.

My father was undoubtedly an exceptional case. This house where I am writing in Talcottville is, I realize, a complete anomaly. In my childhood, it seemed so enchanting, so unlike the rest of my life, that, even in later years, I could hardly, when I was not actually here, believe that it really existed. Now I understand something of the reasons for its seeming so much to belong to a magical world of its own. It was built when this part of the country was only just being opened up for settlement, after a treaty with the Oneida Indians had made it possible for white people to live here. But the first pioneers had so trying a time, with the cold and the lack of supplies, that the government made a temporary ruling that no further land should be sold unless the prospective settler agreed to take in newcomers who had not yet had time to build, and to provide grist for their cattle. The Talcotts were thus engaged in a kind of land speculation. They sold people grist from their mill and building materials from their quarry. The size of the house is accounted for as well as its internal architecture by the necessity of housing a great many people. There used to be outbuildings which have disappeared : a ballroom, a dairy, a quilting room. They made their own candles and nails, and they spun the cloth for their clothes. The place was a town in itself : it was hostelry, town hall and post office, social centre and source of supplies. The line between Lewis and Oneida Counties and a good many other matters were decided beneath this roof. But the speculation did not pan out. The Talcottville pioneers expected to have a railroad run through here, but the railroad passed Talcottville by. The town was supposed to centre about a New England green, on one side of which our house would have stood; but this project was never developed : the "green" is an unused field. The village has remained a small settlement, strung along a relatively unfrequented road. Many members of the family went West; some who stayed here drank far too much and kept on selling pieces of their immense estates. Yet it perfectly pleased my father. It belonged to my mother's family, but he bought it in her name from her uncle and, in his later and darker years, spent as much time as possible here. It was Talcottville he gave her, not Rumson, and at that time she did not want it. The place became, queerly enough, one of the things about which they disagreed. Though it was *her* family who came from here—his own were from central New York (with another stone house in the family background, by that time, I believe, a museum) —it was my father who enjoyed it most. The family reunions of the summer had dwindled to an occasional cousin, and the relatives my mother had liked best were dead. It was depressing for my mother and bored her : she still wanted my father to take her to some place where she could meet new people, where there would be a good deal going on. But he loved the wild country and the solitude; and he had here a devoted friend—one of my mother's connections, a quiet good-humoured man of such imperturbable placidity that one felt it would be difficult for anyone to try to impress him with neurotic complaints—with whom he made countless fishing-trips, sometimes lasting for days, to the cascading rivers and the forested lakes. He liked to talk to the people in the blacksmith shop and the general store, and would sometimes stay an hour while they came and went. When sitting on the vine-screened porch of our house, he would sometimes fall silent when people passed, attentive to what they were saying. He seemed somehow to have made closer connections with the microscopic community of Talcottville than he had ever been able to do in New Jersey. He was elected to the local Grange as an honorary member and enjoyed attending their meetings. He sometimes came up here alone, and, I am told, would give splendid picnics for my mother's remaining relations. Indoors he would occupy himself with the inspection of his fishing tackle or whittle sticks into slender canes that were always finely tapering—I sometimes carry one that he made—or carpenter wooden boxes that were beautifully joined and finished and that he would stain and equip with brass catches —there are several about the house. He would relax here, as I can relax—at home with his own singularity as well as with the village life, at home with the strangeness of this isolated house as well as with the old America that it still represents so solidly.

For the house does today seem strange, and it must always have been rather exceptional. When Washington Irving, at twenty, first visited this part of the country, in the summer of 1803, it was all a romantic wilderness, in which, "at the head of Long Falls [now Carthage]," the best place he could find to lodge was what he called the "Temple of Dirt" of "a little squat Frenchwoman, with a red face, a black wool hat stuck on her head, her hair greasy and her dress and person in similar style. We were heartily glad to make an escape." Yet not many miles from there, this house had been built or was building. It is curious, in reading Irving, to imagine its excellent proportions, its elegance of windows and doorways, its carved fireplaces and branching columns, crystallizing in the forests that the traveller describes. It still seems curious to find it here. In a sense, it has always been stranded. And am I, too, an exceptional case? When, for example, I look through *Life* magazine, I feel that I do not belong to the country depicted there, that I do not even live in that country. Am I, then, in a pocket of the past? I do not necessarily believe it. I may find myself here at the centre of things—since the centre can be only in one's head—and my feelings and thoughts may be shared by many.